Adopting a Child

Amazing Tips on How to Guide a Gifted Child

(Discover Everything You Need to Know About Adopting a Child)

David Andrews

Published By **Darby Connor**

David Andrews

Adopting a Child: Amazing Tips on How to Guide a Gifted Child (Discover Everything You Need to Know About Adopting a Child)

ISBN 978-1-998769-88-9

Table Of Contents

Chapter 1: All Approximately Adoption

Adoption is a manner in which a toddler underneath the age of 18 is permanently located below the care and provision of a discern or parents other than the child's organic parents. It might also both be home or inter-u . S ., however either which have to be arranged with the help of a kingdom corporation or an adoption business enterprise. What is vital, but, is that the adoption corporations, both non-public or public, should have the license to perform in the u . S . Or state.

To be greater different, non-public adoption is one that is arranged among the adoptive parent and the start discern without the resource of an company. This is also referred to as impartial adoption, that is generally settled with the assistance of a lawyer in place of an company, and made manner for the adoption of babies as opposed to kids. In totality, it's miles stated that about fifty five% of all adopted kids within the U.S. Have been settled through impartial adoption. Another type is the public adoption, or one that is

1

organized and processed with the aid of a personal or public organisation, and studies propose that this type of adoption more regularly leads to the adoption of infants or toddlers, instead of older kids.

The phrase adoption has such a lot of nuances that it may be a chunk difficult to pinpoint how most people actually sense about it. In felony phrases, adoption is defined as moving all of the obligations attributed with the care of a baby from the organic parents to every other individual. In maximum adoption cases, as soon because the switch of obligation for the care of the young is entire, the parental rights are transferred to the adopting mother and father as properly. This method that the biological mother and father lose their essential rights to offer the child a safe surroundings to grow up in, in addition to being answerable for the primary duty of offering all of the fundamental wishes of the kid, to develop into a healthful well-adjusted grownup. There are also some instances in which the biological parent is strictly forbidden by the court docket to have any sort of courting with the kid that has already been put up for adoption, specifically if parental rights have already been terminated.

The records of adoption inside the United States is steep with controversy, from the "orphan educate" movement of the past due 1800s to the so-referred to as "child scoop era" of the mid- to overdue 1900s. After a chain of debates and a whole lot of amendments and revisions, US legal guidelines in regards to adoption has eventually turn out to be what it is nowadays. The finalization of America's version for adoption came about at across the 1940s wherein it stated:

The rights of the beginning dad and mom were absolutely severed. This made the adopting couple the followed baby's felony parents in keeping with the regulation. □
Adoption have become a method of making sure the child's excellent hobbies, and □
The whole adoption technique became finished in whole secrecy. This effectively curtailed any possibilities that the adopted toddler would possibly in the future reunite with his or her birth dad and mom unless he

3

or she gets authorization from the courts to open up the unique records of birth. □

With this model, two sorts of adoption emerged, namely:
1. Open adoption – this shape of adoption barely deviates from the system of secrecy stated above. There are a few cases in which the organic and adoptive parents have fashioned a mutual settlement that offers visitation rights to the beginning parents. This may contain other varieties of interaction between the beginning parents and the adopted child, even though the adoptive dad and mom preserve sole custody and complete prison responsibility for the kid. At least 24 US States have allowed this provision within the finalization of adoption papers so long as both parties have given their mutual consent. This settlement is considered binding and legally enforceable.

In addition to visitation and the right of the start parent to achieve statistics about the child, 6 US States have additionally given permission for an followed infant to preserve his original start certificates that remain unaltered no matter the adoption.

4

2. Closed adoption – this adoption process is executed in line with the original version in which the confidentiality of all facts is precisely saved. This means that the identities of the adoptive dad and mom, the biological parents, or the organic kinfolk, who legal the adoption in lieu of the beginning mother and father, are all stored under a good seal of non-disclosure. This practice of adoption is not as established today as it was in the ultimate century.

The decline inside the practice of closed adoption is frequently attributed to recent studies showing that adopted youngsters, who lack a connection in spite of a tiny piece in their pasts, are greater vulnerable to obtaining various mental fitness problems. In addition to that, the shortage of access to the adopted toddler's scientific history, specially the relevant information on any genetic disorders that can had been inherited from the organic parents, is notably damaging to the child's bodily properly-being. In current years, there had been numerous closed adoptions in which non-identifying facts have been allowed to be surpassed over to the adoptive dad and mom, together with the scientific records and the organic parents' ethnic and non secular backgrounds.

Knowing what their alternatives are in terms of adopting a infant has significantly helped plenty of couples take that jump of faith towards bringing a infant of their hearts into their domestic, even if the child isn't associated with both spouse with the aid of blood. It is sufficient to recognise that there's this sincere preference to personal a infant, and that they might need to love and take care of the child, like he/she is certainly one of their personal. No rely what form of adoption a couple might need to have or what shape of adoption, the handiest aspect that matters is that they're able to loving the kid and caring for the child. They are emotionally, bodily, financially capable of fulfill the wishes of the child, to make sure he/she will grow to be a responsible, nurtured individual, who will advantage each the circle of relatives and society. No count number who the child might be, the maximum crucial element is for the figure to reflect over the problems with all their coronary heart and their being, to mirror if they're certainly able to adopting a infant.

Adoption – History and Trends

Adoption has been in life for heaps of years. It has been a practice even about 4,000 years ago, while the Code of Hammurabi in Babylonia became sanctioned in 2285 BC, for parents to care for those who had been no longer their organic children.

Adoption in History And Other Cultures
Mention of or references to the practice can also be seen inside the Hindu Laws of Manu, which was about 2 hundred BC, in addition to within the Bible, when Moses changed into followed by way of the Pharaoh's daughter. The earliest signs of adoption was manifested in Middle Asia, when historical Romans codified the rule of adoption in their legal guidelines. Even Julius Caesar changed into said to have had adopted his nephew Octavian, a good way to hold his dynasty. Adoption became visible over the ages most of the Greeks, Egyptians, Assyrians, Germans, and Japanese amongst others.
In many religions round the world, adoption changed into taken as a sacred requirement, consisting of seen in the Shinto religion, in

7

which there has been ancestral worship and rituals that made manner for the institution of adoption. It was universal as a right that an adopted toddler need to be allowed to carry on the family lineage and rituals, specifically in instances when the couple cannot have organic youngsters. However, in some of these cases found around the world, there has been a not unusual denominator discovered in these kind of instances, which stated that adoption, some thing its motives or intention, satisfies the wishes of both circle of relatives and society. This is due to the fact adoption is beneficial to all of the gamers in the adoption marketplace: from the adoptive mother and father to the relinquishing mother and father to the kid being adopted. For that, it has persevered over time and into the modern-day duration.

The Rise of Adoption in Western Society

Most of the Western societies form their adoption legal guidelines in keeping with the statutes located within the Roman code, or even the latter Napoleonic code. Adoption within the U.S., for instance, has combined the Roman law with its own device. Unlike in Europe, but, wherein felony adoption was most effective took set up someday in 1926 during the Adoption of Children Act, the U.S. Has had adoption laws in vicinity for about one hundred fifty years. There were three tiers, starting with the Massachusetts statute in 1851, whilst more and more orphans and homeless youngsters in States resulted to the need to enact such legal guidelines and set up an adoption gadget for minors, which set the framework for prepared adoptions that would be great for a couple of parties. In the "orphan educate motion" in 1854, as an instance, there had been approximately a hundred,000 homeless kids up until 1904, and most of them have been not formally followed. These remained in the care of the private and public institutions for the duration of the ones years.

The 2nd stage passed off starting in 1920, when the call for for adoption rose rapidly due to the upgrades inside the infant formulation, with the perception that it changed into "nurture"—and not nature— that acted as the principle determinant of baby development. When the expenses of infant system plummeted inside the 1930s, the adoption companies were able to fit more

9

adoptable kids with the adoptive parents, specially due to the fact that some of the adoptive mother and father desired youngsters who have been fit and healthful.

The 1/3 level passed off starting within the Nineteen Sixties, when the variety of adoptable babies declined swiftly, and there had been two additional assets of supply from the listing of overseas-born children, as well as people who have been foster care children. It changed into then that the U.S. Government have become greater liberalized while it came to adoption, until the passage of the Adoption Assistance and Child Welfare Act in 1980, which set up useful adoption assistance applications for each nation, with matching budget that assisted in general the system of adoption.
Adoption Laws Today

It is vital, but, to apprehend that the adoption laws are being evaluated when it comes to their functionality and the present situations of time, or how it's miles being perceived inside the society in relation to how it's far being practiced. There are some of vital factors that have an effect on the system of

10

adoption. This consists of the social, monetary, and political conditions; the societal attitudes towards orphans; the cases of out-of-wedlock births; requirements of parenting; perspectives on parental rights; perspectives on propriety and inheritance; notion on blood ties; as well as non secular and moral values. Partly due to this, it was witnessed that casual adoptions had been the norm of early America, before the passage of the Massachusetts law on adoption.

Informal adoptions are people who occur among the adoptive discern and the relinquishing figure, without court involvement. There had been colonial law that have been being surpassed, spotting the method of adoption of a baby. However, as illegitimacy turned into taken as some thing evil, adoption changed into greater targeted at the adoptive figure, in preference to the kid being adopted. This went until the case of Mary Ellen Wilson entered the public in 1874. Mary become an followed baby who turned into critically beaten and abused through her adoptive parents, and it raised cognizance and encouraged the public to recognition extra at the adoptive child, as opposed to the

11

adoptive determine. By then, New York's Society for the Prevention of Cruelty to Children became the primary enterprise inside the global to protect kids from being abused. The interest switched to children and their rights to residing a healthful and happy life after the adoption.

During early 20th century, modern-day adoption remains greater on casual in preference to criminal though. When the primary expert conference in adoption turned into held in 1955 by means of the Child Welfare League of America, the fashion persevered to favor casual adoption, especially due to the fact residents could not see the advantage of making use of for legal adoption, except for the availability of inheritance to the child. However, after World War II, adoption companies grew in variety and became extra distinguished, making manner for felony adoption to take region greater often in lots of States throughout america. During this era, children who had had nobody to care for them have been taken to orphanages or orphan asylums, till involved parents determine to take the child of their care. During such length, there has been much less confidentiality with regards to the identities of the birthparents and the followed infant. As the courts began to handle most of the adoption approaches, ensuring that parties are protected, there emerged the adoption marketplace, and nowadays, the adoption appears extra like a system of production and governance.

Chapter 2: Adopting A Child For The First Time... Where To Start?

It is ordinary for mother and father who are considering adoption for the first time to have loads of questions in their minds. It is crucial to address these questions even earlier than searching out a toddler that they could likely undertake. The couple who want to adopt might additionally need to deeply explore their reasons for considering, to make sure that, what they do could be the best factor for the kid to revel in. Why? Because kids who've been put up for adoption are often those, whose possibilities of having a strong existence with their biological mother and father, are near not anything. These kids regularly live from one sadness to any other, and adoption is their most effective desire of salvation.

The following lists down some of the most not unusual motives for adoption within the US:
 Infertility. According to statistics, at least 1 out eight couples in the US is unable to get pregnant because one or each are infertile.

14

The majority of these couples opt to satisfy their want for an offspring via adoption. □

Pregnancy poses a first-rate medical threat both for the mom or the fetus. In a few instances, both the mom and the fetus are at risk so couples opt to undertake as an alternative. □

Single humans may also want to enjoy life as a discern however no longer as a married individual. □

Same intercourse couples may additionally need to have a own family however are not able to have a baby within the traditional manner. However, there are cases while gay couples donate sperms to a surrogate mother who incorporates the child up to maturity in her womb. The surrogate can also or won't be a part of the kid's upbringing relying on her agreement with the 'fathers'. □

Couples who're already raising a circle of relatives might also desire to increase it through adoption. Often, the couple can also already be past the secure toddler-bearing age. But within the case of famous Hollywood couple Brad Pitt and Angelina Jolie, they really wanted to have a massive brood, maximum of whom come from 0.33-international countries in which the kid's probabilities of survival and a cushty way of life is very low. ☐

While it's miles real that adopting a baby can convey first rate pleasure to a parent, it also explores a number of u.S.And downs, which the figure ought to apprehend conveniently, specially for the reason that time right now after the adoption is seemed as the maximum important, tough time for both the kid and the discern, and it would remain a project for some time. Therefore, step one whilst making plans to adopt a infant is to invite your self the motive why you need to undertake. Those who are seeking to adopt a infant ought to take a look at the factors which have come to motivate them.

There are some of motives that potential parents pick out to adopt a baby, and amongst them are the instances of infertility, preference to have larger households, choice to help a child, or choice to do social justice, or make a contribution to society. As in the case of infertility, for example, those type of parents have usually gone thru a curler coaster of emotions, of hopes and despairs, of demanding situations and hopelessness.

16

Those who have had repeated miscarriages or intrusive fertility treatments might also experience grief over their loss, not to mention emotions of inadequacy and lack of control. Thus, it'd be for the good of all if those mother and father might method guide agencies and counselors before trying to undertake a toddler. Because human beings do now not usually come to a decision at the identical time or place, then there may be an offended accomplice who may also have no longer yet considered accepting most of these and goes over a feeling of grief. Before going via a choice making process, make sure that the partners are bodily, emotionally, mentally able to what is set to take vicinity. Make positive they are in shape and ready to add one more infant into the circle of relatives, and they could be pleased to spend time with the child, that the future may be one that is agreeable and satisfying.

The next step after going over the selection is to determine on some factors, such as the age of the kid, the gender of the child, the cultural identity of the kid, and the region wherein the child comes from. The mother and father should have interaction in some self-

17

reflection on how the child will fit into their lives, and the lives in their families, how it'll affect the own family dynamics, in particular if there are organic kids as nicely. Reflect at the changes that needed to be carried out, for a higher transition of the child into the family. The parents need to reflect on whether or not they're inclined to entertain open adoption wherein adoptive mother and father make personal touch with the organic mother and father. Are they inclined to simply accept kids who got here from orphanages or the foster care systems, in which kids may additionally have had experienced being abused or omitted? If they want a transracial adoption, then how would they accommodate or promote the kid's racial identification while the kid comes to be of age? Do they recognise how or where they could searching for assist for themselves and for their adopted child as soon as it will become vital? All these questions could be beneficial to parents earlier than coming to a choice about adopting a foster child.

During adoption, be very conscious on the effect no longer just to the child however to the adoptive determine as well. They have to reflect onconsideration on the impact that the act might lead upon, and don't forget that it is very critical for the figure to be happy with their selection after the adoption is made. They need to make sure that they will now not remorse adopting a infant, and that they're conveniently capable of giving love and assistance to the child. Studies imply that a remarkable majority of adoptive mother and father are happy with their selection. However, the query is whether they may remain satisfied months or years after the adoption method had been settled. The postadoption duration provides its difficulties inside the case of the parents, and that they have to recognize that adoption is a existence-long procedure. Among the possibilities are the tendency for the determine to enjoy melancholy after the adoption procedure. This might also name for what's called "postadoption despair syndrome", which may additionally arise within a few weeks after the adoption is finalized. Another possibility are the instances associated with identity and attachment, as some dad and mom can be ignorant of what's predicted of them because the adoptive parent. In those instances, it's far advocated

19

to hook up with different dad and mom who have experienced the identical component. It would also be properly to set up own family traditions, and to connect with the start way of life of the kid. Nothing is better than to be mindful of the situation in every little element, even to people who relate to the little information that have been usually left out.

Issues on the Type of Adoption

Now that the couple has determined their primary purpose for deciding on to adopt a baby, the following query is: how do prospective dad and mom pass about the adoption system? The first issue to do is to select the shape of adoption. Would the couple be amenable to an open adoption or would they be more snug with the closed adoption procedure? This selection can be made through understanding the benefits and drawbacks of every shape of adoption, each open adoption and closed adoption.

Nowadays, there's the fashion for open adoption, in which the start discern is given the privilege of maintaining contact or relation with the kid, even after the adoption is finalized. There are already rights given to the start mom, who's privileged with the right to select the family or man or woman who might adopt the child. These open adoption agreements usually take form in mediated adoptions, as well as those that take region in the foster care. Meanwhile, communication is also maintained in open adoption between the start figure and the adoptive parent, despite the fact that it can vary in phrases of the way regularly the verbal exchange takes location, in addition to in which, while, and who is given the authority to speak with the kid. There will also be a few periodic exchanges of letters, pix, or notes among the delivery circle of relatives and the adoptive own family, no longer to mention the privilege of being capable of visit the kid within the adoptive circle of relatives, both for the duration of ordinary days or during festivities or occasional days. With this, open adoption carries some of blessings, in particular in phrases of the adoptive dad and mom.

Open adoption has the subsequent advantages:

• The adopted child gets to maintain a few kind of dating with his beginning parents until the child grows old.

• The adoptive mother and father might be able to talk directly with the birth mother and father. This is an important element of understanding the kid's attitude and emotional responses to certain conditions considering the fact that those should probably be inherited.

• There is availability of clinical records in case the adopted toddler figures in an emergency.

• The adoptive mother and father could also be capable of gain a higher know-how of why the delivery mother and father had to supply the child up for adoption. This in turn might give them enough statistics on a way to nicely deal with the questions that the kid would certainly have as quickly as he grows old enough to understand that he is adopted.

In the interim, studies display that open adoption could be very useful not simply to the adoptive child but to all who're worried. It takes away the mystery and curiosity at the facet of the kid, and the sorrow at the facet of the birth discern. It takes away the fear and loneliness, and can largely be beneficial on the sole identity of the delivery determine and the kid. Openness is said to be associated with better postadoption adjustment to each the birth determine and the adoptive determine. With open adoption, they can make sure that there's higher adjustment for all who're worried, and with non-stop touch, they could receive more willingly the future effects.

A key downside of open adoption is the opportunity that the delivery parents would possibly someday become too ahead in stressful for more time to be spent with the kid. There is likewise the opportunity that unsupervised visits between the birth parents and the followed infant could develop into a means for the start parents to attempt to turn the kid towards his adoptive parents. However, this has rarely befell since the terms for maximum open adoptions have been arranged even earlier than the beginning of the child. In maximum cases, the beginning dad and mom additionally get to pick out to whom they could want to entrust their baby's upbringing. With open adoption, there may be more openness and connectedness among

23

the adopted baby and the delivery determine. However, it can lead to a few issues on the side of the adoptive figure, which can reduce their authority in formulating the destiny of the adopted baby. It may also flip out that the child grows to abandon the adoptive parents due to an excessive amount of have an effect on and association with the delivery parents. It is satisfactory consequently, to adjust how often the kid comes into touch with his/her delivery parents, and for how long should it take. There are others who allow the relationship in the course of the years of formative years, after which restrict the time at some stage in early life. The motive is for the child to understand his/her proper identity, which must have taken place at some point of childhood or early adulthood.

With regard to closed adoption, there's limited statistics about the delivery discern of the adopted infant, as well as their racial and cultural heritage. This normally takes location throughout inter-united states of america adoption, in which the youngsters usually arrive as infants or infants. There are also instances while the adoptive toddler is on its primary years. However, the primary denominator in this type of instances is that, kids who're followed through inter-country adoption commonly consist of individuals who are put in foster care because of negative aspects, such as parental abuse, forget, parental substance abuse, abandonment, and poverty. In all these, there is typically best little reliable information in terms of the child's history, clinical records, in addition to the household of the child. Children who are adopted thru closed adoption need a wonderful deal extra from the adoptive dad and mom, seeing that there's nearly nothing that they might understand approximately the child earlier than being put in their care. There may likewise be some of adoption issues that they will must cope with, to make certain that the child grows in fitness and glad surroundings, whilst going over the developmental ranges of youth greater efficaciously. In a closed adoption, there's interest and worry in the system, and the adoptive mother and father have to be geared up and extra inclined to accept the various challenges that is soon to take region, whilst the child inquires about his/her genuine identification.

25

Choosing the Right Path that Leads to Adoption

There are four number one paths that couples can take in relation to choosing a baby of their hearts, and those are:

1. Domestic adoption business enterprise – this is the maximum not unusual way for acquiring an open adoption since the organization frequently works intently with delivery moms in selecting feasible adoptive dad and mom for the unborn infant. Couples who are interested in adopting a child are required to post their info to the domestic organization. These are then reviewed and handed directly to the start mothers. Once the biological mother has made her desire, it's far then time for the organization to ensure that the adoption manner goes easily. Domestic adoption organizations may also facilitate a meeting between the feasible adoptive mother and father and the mom wherein both parties are given the risk to shape a relationship that would be beneficial for the unborn baby. There aren't that many home organizations inside the US that also offer aid for couples who desire to go through a closed adoption manner considering the

26

fact that most start moms are regularly unwilling to consider entire confidentiality.

2. Independent adoption – through this direction, couples are capable of discover applicants for adoption with the aid of a legal professional or a medical doctor. These intermediaries are in price of finding a beginning mom who's inclined to place her infant up for adoption, or discover possible adoptive dad and mom for a delivery mother who has to put the unborn infant up for adoption. These intermediaries paintings with both the adoptive dad and mom or the start mother though they're not related with any home adoption organization. It is essential for adoptive mother and father and beginning moms to first verify the legal guidelines that pertain to independent adoption in their localities. The following States have declared impartial adoption to be illegal:
a. Connecticut
b. Delaware
c. Massachusetts
d. Minnesotta

In most cases, the adoptive dad and mom are required to cowl all costs that are associated with the adoption, which includes:

• The price for locating the possible beginning mom.

• The beginning mom's being pregnant and delivery costs, including visits to the health practitioner, vitamins, and many others.

• Fees that want to be paid for the legal documents of the adoption, as well as the lawyer or the mediator who is supporting the couple.

A few states have legalized the technique of the adoptive parents procuring the living charges of the delivery mom as much as a positive point. When a lot of these prices are summed up, the overall bill for impartial adoption frequently reaches USD$10,000 and higher, although some couples might be able to avail of a credit score for federal adoption tax.

3. Foster care – that is desired by couples who want to adopt a child who is already at the 'waiting list' for adoption. The simplest way for couples to find a potential followed infant thru foster care is by means of going online to test the database. There are hundreds of

profiles and photographs that adoptive parents can browse through if you want to locate that one infant that they can in the end call their own. However, there are a few matters that couples have to take note whilst thinking about adoption via the foster care machine, including:

a. Couples have to go through the local employer that handles the foster care in order to coordinate the viable adoption of a baby. These are the equal corporations that offer the online listing for waiting youngsters.

b. Children in foster care have had to spend some time in the machine, so they are extra frequently emotionally unstable. Couples who are inclined to adopt a toddler from foster care must be equipped to cope with the emotional united statesand downs that the kid might bring with him. They should be ready to provide a loving domestic where the child could be accepted for what he is and nurtured to grow into a nicely-balanced individual. Some of those kids have suffered one shape of abuse or any other, so adoptive mother and father must discover ways to aid the child that they undertake within the method of recovery from his wounds.

29

c. Infants on waiting lists inside the foster care device are few and far among. Couples should be ready to select a toddler from a waiting list of kids that might already be of their young adults. Adopting a person who has already shaped his own set of beliefs approximately the sector he lives in may be more difficult than adopting an unborn baby. Therefore, the adoptive parents need to be emotionally and mentally organized when they decide to adopt a teenager.

Each country corporation has its very own website in which profiles of the waiting children within the foster care system are posted for potential dad and mom to view.

Couples can also select to discover a baby to adopt by way of seeking the useful resource of a private adoption corporation or by using looking at international adoption alternatives. The latter has clearly emerge as a piece of a trend for Hollywood celebrities within the beyond few years. It isn't unusual to listen of a superstar who adopted a child or a few youngsters one after the other from a conflict-torn and impoverished us of a. Probably the maximum sensational of those celebrity adoptions is located inside the legality of Madonna's baby adoption, despite the fact that the case did get taken care of out in due time.

There are also some instances in which step-parents are inquisitive about legally adopting their stepchildren. In those times, they would ought to seek advice from an adoption attorney or consult their neighborhood courtroom with reference to the approaches that they might to undergo so as to finish the adoption procedure. They may wish to get preserve of the adoption worksheet for step-dad and mom that is provided by the Children Welfare Information Gateway for a step-by way of-step guide at the adoption method. The same is actual for relatives, such as grandparents, aunts, or uncles, who want to adopt an orphaned relative or every other infant from the foster care.

31

Chapter 3: Going Through A

Private/Independent Adoption

The blessings and downsides of pursuing adoption with the resource of an organization, whether or not it's far nation-run or personal, are pretty apparent already. It isn't any surprise that most couples opt to choose their adoptive infant from an organization's listing. Independent or non-public adoption is also now not as popular as the opposite paths because it isn't prison in all US states and each nation has its very own legal guidelines touching on this method. For the sake of readability, it's far higher to examine all the options for adoption greater deeply, so here's a list of the benefits that might be gained from unbiased adoption:

• The potential mother and father have a bigger chance of in my opinion meeting the possible start mother and father. This offers both events the possibility to have their questions replied individually through the other, and that they get to agree on adoption phrases that could be most beneficial no longer best for them however additionally

32

normally for the unborn child. Remember, the intention of adoption isn't to give the birth mother and father extra freedom to live their stay or to offer the potential mother and father a baby to like as their personal. Adoption is always approximately doing what is pleasant for the child before he is even born.

• Couples who're in a rush to find a infant to adopt also get to keep away from the waiting lists which are a commonplace exercise in agency-assisted adoption and trough the foster care gadget. This is most usually beneficial for couples who already recognize of a pregnant teenager who needs to place her unborn infant up for adoption or any person else close to them who isn't equipped to end up a discern yet.

• Independent adoption is likewise quicker than organization-assisted or foster care adoption. From the moment that a search is began for a potential beginning mom till the adoption papers are approved, it generally simply takes approximately a year or .

• Couples might be able to store a couple of bucks through unbiased adoption, including the agency charge that is usually a requirement when searching for the help of

33

an company for the adoption. Except for this, all different fees are the identical, and the couple ought to apply for the federal adoption tax credit score should they wish to.

There are several methods that couples can execute the unbiased adoption manner. Those who already realize of a infant that they could in all likelihood adopt are luckier than maximum on account that all they could want to worry about is getting the adoption papers accredited by means of the court. However, couples who are nonetheless in the dark as to wherein they could discover a child can do the subsequent steps, with the aid of an authorized mediator of route:

1. Advertise within the neighborhood paper about the goal for adopting a infant or someone who is but to be born. These advertisements can be run privately, and the start mother and father are given the choice to both contact the possible dad and mom immediately or contact the mediator first.

2. Make use of personal referral services and adoption listings which might be run via private placement companies.

3. Make use of the diverse adoption facilitation services that abound on the

internet. These websites offer prospective parents and beginning moms a manner to discover every other thru a carrier that matches their profiles.

Once the couple reveals a infant, the subsequent element to do is to fill-out all the essential bureaucracy that would finalize the adoption. These bureaucracy are available on the county clerk's office or on line on the kingdom court's website. Another reminder, though: always test what the nearby court docket's ruling is in regards to impartial adoption. Most states require that the kid be placed within the prospective parents' domestic for a while earlier than the adoption method ought to start. For a higher know-how of every state's legal guidelines touching on independent adoption, it is first-class to appearance it up on the e-book State Statutes that are sent out via the United States Department of Health and Human Services.

Once the nation regulation is virtually understood, the adoption can now start to run its due route. Everyone concerned inside the adoption system could ought to signal certain files, maximum of which might be distinctive for the role that each person is playing. However, the following paperwork have to be collectively filled out by each the adoptive dad and mom and the delivery mother and father:

Adoption Application shape, also called the Petition for Adoption☐

Consent of beginning mother is she remains alive, and/or the birth father if his whereabouts is known☐

Consent of the kid. Infants and youngsters up to the age of 12 are exempt from this rule. Some states, but, require the adoptive parents to reap the child's consent if he's 12 years vintage and above. Without this, the adoption cannot continue. ☐

Petition to waive the sponsorship of an organisation. ☐

Adoption Decree. This is the very last step for the adoption procedure. The adoptive dad and mom are required to record this earlier than a decide hears the case at final hearing. Once the choose presents the adoption, he could then put his signature on the Order of Decree. This makes the adoption legal and binding.☐

Once all the bureaucracy were completely filled-out, the prospective parents must post it to the clerk of court docket. The subsequent step is to set up for the prices and the house examine. These are requirements for adoption court cases in each unmarried one of the US states, despite the fact that each State has its personal laws concerning adoption. This may be mentioned similarly in the proceeding chapters.

Requirements - Adoption Fees

As in another criminal matter, prospective dad and mom who desire to undertake a toddler from any of the aforementioned paths mentioned in Chapter three have several necessities that need to be met. It is constantly exceptional to bear in mind that adoption legal guidelines range according to country, so couples ought to first check with their kingdom organizations so one can verify the nation-particular criteria for adoption. With regard to personal characteristics, adoptive dad and mom must be:
• Stable
• Mature
• Flexible

• Dependable

It is also a ought to for potential dad and mom in an effort to recommend for kids's rights because they might simply be letting a infant who is not related to both of them by using blood into their homes. Without the right mind-set, adoption may want to change into some thing this is even more traumatizing for the followed toddler than foster care.

Couples who're searching into their alternatives for adoption additionally must put together themselves for the prices that the whole adoption procedure would clearly incur. Aside from fees on the pregnancy and delivery of the kid, different fees that ought to be minded are:

Home examine price☐
Legal prices☐
Travel charges for youngsters from a specific locality☐

There are many locations where dad and mom can undertake a baby, as there are a number of groups and establishments that quite simply serve mother and father who want to undertake a baby. Each of these agencies end result to a extraordinary set of costs, and it may vary from as high as $50,000 to as low as nothing at all, depending on how the child is being adopted, as well as the kind of adoption.

The maximum cost-effective manner of adopting a toddler is to take them from foster care. In the year 2012, there has been predicted number of fifty two,039 children in the U.S. Who have been waiting to be followed by using interested dad and mom. It is generally the state businesses that handle the processing of adoption from the foster care, despite the fact that there are a couple of ways wherein interested mother and father can undertake.

First is through at once applying for adoption in the foster care; and second is via becoming foster mother and father first before adopting the child, the time after the rights of the delivery parents had been terminated. In foster care, followed kids commonly fall on the age of 7.8 years antique, and maximum of them have special wishes in phrases of the physical, behavioral, or mental disabilities, as well as in terms of age or courting to a minority organization. The traditional value tiers from $zero to $three,000 that could cowl the preliminary expenses. The charges may be recovered by using federal reimbursement plan or thru using an adoption tax credit, regardless of what the real fees are.

Next in line for a more low-budget technique of adopting a child is to do it privately. In doing so, the adoptive discern has to discover the potential start determine. Lawyers can be helpful in this level, as they can control the processing of adoption, even without the assist of adoptive corporations. In reality, in an estimated wide variety of 18,000 new child adoptions, half of them were completed privately or independently with out the want for adoptive organizations. There is, but, a technique of doing this. First, the unbiased adopters could send resumés to attorneys and obstetricians. Second, they put it up for sale what they may be looking for in newspaper labeled sections or in Web pages and blogs for them to suit their specifics with a start parent. Third, arrange for a plan to satisfy with the delivery parents of the adoptive toddler, and be prepared for health center stay and ongoing touch. After this, the

40

adoptive parent can take the kid domestic at once from the medical institution. The fee for adopting a infant privately and independently tiers from $7,000 to $10,000 for use in paying felony costs for each the adoptive parents and the birth mother and father. There might be a further cost of approximately $7,500 for the clinical prices, and this will general to an approximate value of $25,000 in totality, as there are different fees in caring for the child.

Next is by way of adopting a baby from an adoption agency. The adoptive mother and father would only should contact an adoption company and set their criteria for the interested candidates. Before, they do it through putting their names on a listing and then awaiting a match. Nowadays, however, there's more openness and connection between the adoptive mother and father and the start parents, and the former are likely to fulfill the birth dad and mom in my opinion. It is likewise suited for the start dad and mom to request to look their child in the destiny and preserve touch. The organisation might then ship a few discern profiles to the beginning dad and mom, who would then select the mother and father whom they would want their child to be with. This way that as opposed to the adoptive mother and father selecting the adoptive baby, fashion has it that, it is now the birth dad and mom who would pick out the adoptive parent for his or her baby, while the employer tries to match both standards. Open adoption typically takes place inside the foster care or in hospitals right now after the birth of the kid. In closed adoption, however, the birth parents might also should wait longer, considering the fact that maximum of the adoption groups nowadays cross for openness in adoption. In adopting a baby from adoption groups, the typical value tiers from $20,000 to $40,000, which incorporates the home take a look at, the counseling, the scientific prices, in addition to the foster care (if wanted). Fees are predictable regardless of the carrier or aid is.

Last but now not the least is via adopting a child internationally via inter-united states of america adoption. In 2013, Americans had adopted a total of 7,092 kids from other countries overseas like the ones in Asia, Eastern Europe, Africa, or Latin America. Most of these inter-usa adoptions are being handled with the aid of ideal U.S.-based organizations, as they are capable of take care of adoptions from unique international locations, together with the US. The corporation connects with a setting organisation overseas, which might also both be a governmental body, a non-public orphanage, a social welfare group, or a basis. Still, there are some of countries who require the adoptive parent to tour to their united states first and recognise their guidelines on the subject of adoption earlier than selecting up the child. However, in terms of inter-united states of america adoption, the adoptive mother and father ought to be prepared to deal with some issues with the child, along with undernourishment, developmental delays, or emotional problems amongst others. With this, adoptive parents typically consult a doctor first, to check the child's fitness facts and recognize the desires of the kid. The standard price for inter-country adoption tiers from $25,000 to $50,000 or maybe extra, and it generally depends on the tour necessities and country necessities where the child is to be adopted. The risks centers on the time it takes to look ahead to office work needed from the U.S.

Authorities and the companion country, no longer to say the clinical information that is to be despatched to the adoptive parents.

Chapter 4: Requirements - Home Study

Home observe is only required in any type of adoption, whether or not it's far closed or open adoption, privately or with the help of an organization. Home study involves education, training, and gathering of facts, which might be useful to the adoptive parents, as they cross over the processing of adoption. It can take from 2 months to about 10 months, which would depend initially on the waiting lists of the agency, not to say the training necessities, which could vary from one nation to every other. Thus, the adoptive dad and mom need to check at the State Adoption Program to realize the specific rules of their State. This is likewise applied in inter-u . S . Adoption, and the adoptive dad and mom might also have to learn about the particular rules observed within the u . S . From wherein the adoptive child could come from.

The domestic study price needs to be shouldered via the potential mother and father on the grounds that they are required by way of regulation to have their homes

45

screened before the adoption can be concluded. Home observe has the ultimate goal of determining what is satisfactory for the kid by means of verifying whether or not the adoptive dad and mom are living a life this is suitable for a kid or no longer. Some of the things which might be checked on for the duration of the home study consist of:

- Each potential determine's family background
- Employment history
- Background test for any criminal information
- Credit take a look at
- Background test of each parent's medical records
- Any acknowledged cases of abuses that become administered by using both of the potential dad and mom
- Home situations together with sanitation and hearth protection compliance

In a home look at, all the candidates for the adoption need to be protected, whether they're single or married, or both as couples who are adopting mutually. In the 21 States in the U.S., an grownup member of the household have to first be evaluated with the

46

aid of the enterprise earlier than they can be normal as an applicant. There are a total of nineteen States round America that require all of the household contributors of the family, no matter age, to be included within the home examine, and this includes youngsters who're under 7 years of age and adults who are past 60 years of age.

The home observe might decide the type of community from where the kid might in all likelihood grow up, as well as the level of understanding of the prospective dad and mom, especially considering the relationship that they could have to establish with the followed infant. These relationships are fantastically exceptional from the connection that mother and father proportion with their organic youngsters, especially if the followed baby have been undernourished, omitted, or abused. This is because adopted youngsters commonly yield bigger emotional luggage at the aspect of dad and mom, whilst in comparison with different children.

The home study is conducted by way of a licensed social worker and/or a representative of the adoption business enterprise. There are State laws that

47

designate the tips for someone who is apt to conduct a domestic take a look at—person who could be appropriate to the courtroom at some stage in the adoption petition. This is typically performed via certified baby-adopting organisation or a person who's being distinct via the courtroom to conduct the home study. Beforehand, relevant certificate may additionally be required, inclusive of records of beginning and marriage. In maximum cases, the house take a look at team could additionally have to talk with the prospective mother and father' personal references so that you can decide the couple's viability for adoption. Only while the home have a look at has been finished and an approval rating is furnished can the couple begin to go searching for a kid whom they can undertake.

However, there are reigning qualifications for any man or woman who needs to be an adoptive determine. In Maryland and New Hampshire, a pair that wishes to undertake a infant must gift an proof of a solid marriage, at the same time as there are 4 States that require the couple to be married for a minimum length of time. New York requires

48

at least 1 12 months of marriage. Mississippi and Arkansas require 2 years of marriage. Alabama requires 3 years of marriage. Meanwhile, there are five States that don't permit adoption to couples that are not legally married, which include Arkansas, Louisiana, Mississippi, Nevada, and Utah. In addition, the adoptive dad and mom have to also be in desirable health, and has ok income to fulfill the wishes of the adoptive child. Home possession isn't always being required, even though they have to have at the least a history of strong residence over time, that can accommodate correctly and securely. There are 13 States that require the adoptive parents to have finished a circle of relatives education training first from a selected adoption corporation or branch discovered inside the specific State. However, it is under the regulation that no applicant of adoption can be excluded from consideration, whether in terms of sex, race, countrywide starting place, or faith. Still, Alabama and New Mexico require that the applicant should be at least a U.S. Citizen, or at least a respective resident of the State.

In a home examine, the objective is to ensure that the adoptive parents are able to making a lifelong commitment to the kid, and they are able to offer a nurturing domestic and own family. In instances in which the adoptive parents have already selected the child, the home study will then check whether or not the adoptive parents can meet the unique desires of the child. This is very vital, especially in cases while the adoptive infant is taken from the foster care or from another usa, and there are issues in fitness or in conduct. For this, the accomplishing agent will interview the candidates, such as all of the circle of relatives participants, to collect insights on whether the adoptive dad and mom are certainly capable. This could check their parenting competencies, their attitudes towards adoption, their personal attitudes, and their social characteristics. The agent is more likely to gather non-public references as well for further records. There will probable be onsite domestic visits, to make sure the house is secure, snug, and secured, with conformity to the neighborhood building codes. Many States additionally require the adoptive mother and father to post their current fitness examinations, to make sure that they're in shape sufficient to display the child. They may also take a look at the papers for criminal statistics or toddler abuse or records of overlook and incapacity. An adoptive parent who is located to were convicted with crime will not be established by means of courtroom.

What Every Parent has to Know approximately Adoption

Say the Order of Decree is signed and the followed baby has ultimately been brought domestic to be brought to his new family, what do dad and mom must do subsequent? Does their duty quit with taking the kid home? The answer is a particular no. A discern's duty starts the day the kid is conceived in the womb and would handiest quit while the discern is six toes underneath. Since adoption is basically taking full duty for a teenager who may or might not be associated with the adoptive dad and mom by using blood, it approach that the parents have agreed to be mother and father to that infant for as long as they probably may want to. Once the adoption papers are authorized, they turn out to be the kid's primary supply of parental guide, and that they come to be answerable for the child's health and nicely-being. Their responsibility begins once they take the child to their home.

Most adoptive dad and mom often find themselves in a predicament as to when the proper time is for telling the kid that he is followed. In the case of an open adoption, the child already becomes privy to the dynamics of his own family early on since his start parents are obliged to shape a courting with him. But this isn't constantly the case in every adoption. And despite the fact that the child already is aware of he's adopted from day 1 that does not suggest that everybody can grow to be snug with the reputation quo. Adoptive mother and father have bigger duties ahead of them.

These include:
1. Parents ought to prepare in each component to acquire the followed infant into their domestic. An adoption isn't always most effective approximately doing all the necessary paperwork and assembly all of the country-imposed necessities. It is likewise approximately being psychologically prepared

to take on the responsibilities of turning into a determine to an adopted baby, in addition to confronting any terrible feelings that might result in a warfare with the child inside the future. And being emotionally organized means information that adoption is not a way to make amends for infertility or the loss of biological youngsters. It is simply a way of expanding the family.

In order to acquire the right stage of mental and emotional preparedness, mother and father should continuously train themselves with reference to adoption. It could also help if adoptive parents are capable of find a support institution of their community, with whom they can percentage their triumphs and trials with. An adoptive circle of relatives can benefit largely from a set of those who understand the scenario in a manner that no different organization can. It is likewise vital for parents to look for a help organization for his or her adopted toddler/youngsters.

2. The experiences of an followed baby are real. Trying to relieve an adopted child's struggling by sweeping the whole thing below the rug does no longer assist at all. Adoptive parents ought to apprehend that, just like

every other infant, adopted children also need validation for their emotions. They want to grow up in an environment wherein they could effectively discover their feelings approximately being followed. Adopted youngsters need to pave their futures with the aid of coming to phrases with their pasts. In order for them to grow into emotionally-balanced adults, they first need to confront their emotions of rejection via their organic mother and father. It is the adoptive determine's activity to assist the child in know-how why he was put up for adoption and to make the kid experience that he is exactly in which he must be: in a loving home with loving dad and mom.

three. Adoptive dad and mom must take into account that it is good enough to hold repeating their child's story time and again once more. As one movie manufacturer wrote on her blog, her followed youngsters surely love hearing the story of how they first met, till they ultimately fixated on sure elements of the story that have become their favorites. This regular repetition makes it less complicated for the child to turn the enjoy into an integrated part of his character.

Moreover, these memories would supply the child something to preserve directly to at some stage in the instances when his friends start to question his being followed. By constantly repeating the adoption tale to the child, the parents can impart in him a sense of who he's. Parents would should be cautious approximately the phrases that they use in telling these testimonies, though. It is vital now not to make the kid feel like he was responsible for the situation that led as much as his birth mom placing him up for adoption. Is it higher to apply phrases that aren't loaded with an excessive amount of which means however are able to bring the determine's love for and recognition of the kid.

At this stage, it's miles apparent that adoption calls for a lot of hard work, a number of effort at the discern's part to put together and to validate the adopted toddler's region within the own family. This is why adoption isn't always constantly advocated for every couple who misplaced a infant to contamination, or who's not able to conceive a child for anything reason. In the quit, files and charges are the very best and more negligible parts of the adoption system. What actually makes a

55

distinction is how the mother and father build their adopted child's lifestyles and their willingness to make sacrifices for his/her first-class pastimes. They have to have the willingness to proportion their lives with a infant, bringing him/her to better existence, with all the comfort and requirements that they could supply the child. In most of these, there must be love and sincerity from the aspect of the adoptive mother and father, as those positivity could be manifested to the child in many than one thousand methods. Much of all, there must be acceptance, with out a greed nor hate, for the kid to develop up in higher country. For the adoptive figure, they have to be reminded that their sole motive, in a single manner or every other, is to offer the kid with a better way of living, to give the kid a better own family, a better destiny, a higher world to stay in.

Adoption from the Inside Out

There are a terrific wide variety of psychoanalytic clinicians who suggested that, in terms of adoption, it's miles better but to preserve adoption a mystery to be stored from the child, specially if the kid is below 7 years of age. Studies have shown that children who are not yet 7 years vintage still do not undergo normal improvement, and it can inflict a mental injury to the child, making way for inner emotional and cognitive problems. These kids are nevertheless under the developmental period of latency, and it can cause ache, sadness, and mourning on the side of the kid. In the play of Albee, entitled "Who's Afraid of Virginia Woolf?", the instant where the history of adoption is found out to a toddler may be likened to a deadly stressful telegram, and it's far unrightful to reveal it, no longer unless the adoptive dad and mom have shaped a sincere, loving dating with the kid. To inform the child that he/she has been adopted, there must in most cases be proper dating among the determine and the kid, so it ends in a feeling of emotional safety and belongingness.

Adoption can impose psychological pressure on every of the participants: the relinquishing dad and mom, the adoptive parents, and the adopted infant. These stresses, however, are detrimentally connected to human impulses, inclusive of sexuality, aggression, procreation, and rivalry, so that it impacts the fundamental human relationships among spouses or between discern and child. As for the case of the kid, there is a sense of longing, wondering that the days of happiness, when his father changed into the noblest of all guys and his mother the dearest of all ladies, appeared to disappear in the air. By this, the child turns faraway from his/her father of the previous day to his/her father of nowadays, and the thought might best linger in the mind of the child—a remorse that the ones satisfied days are long gone.

For that reason, many parents have decided not simply to adopt a child, but to assist the child in whatever challenges he/she may work thru. Only one motive stays after the adoption of a child: to behave humanely as genuine discern to the kid. While it's far authentic that adoption blessings the child greater, it can't be ignored but, that adoption can also do wonders for the adoptive discern. Having a baby ends in happiness and affection, considering parenthood—despite the fact that difficult—can cause a country past delight. As Freud once reminded his readers,

"In developing and loving our kids, we re-create and love part of ourselves. We provide to our kids the task of pleasurable the goals that we had been not capable of satisfy, and insofar as they're capable of acquire what we have needed for them, they gratify our personal desires for ourselves."

With parental love, a brand new connection is born, as an undesirable infant is joined to a figure trying for a kid to like and to take care of. There isn't any undesirable child within the international of adoptive mother and father, for they do love the child inasmuch as they could love their personal.

Chapter 5: Decision-Making In Adoption

There may be varying motives why a circle of relatives or a pair could want to lodge to adoption to elevate a kid. Some households would like to feature some other family member and choose adoption to meet the want. Some couples just passed off to be unable to provide their personal offspring even as others just wanted to help abandoned children. These are simply some of the possible conditions that might push humans to recollect adoption.

Whatever the cause behind adoption, one need to not forget that that is a chief selection that have to be thought of carefully. There are numerous factors that have to be considered earlier than selecting the matter. Adoption will convey main change in the own family's life; therefore, finding out as a own family might be important. There have to be a sizeable and objective self-reflection for the adoptive mother and father before pursuing the technique. The motives why they need to adopt have to be crystal clear to them.

The following are questions taken from Child Welfare Information Gateway, Children's

Bureau/Administration on Children, Youth and Family in an effort to be of terrific assist for couples and households planning to pursue adoption.

- How will a brand new baby suit into the mother and father' lives and their courting?
- How will a brand new infant affect circle of relatives dynamics—particularly if the own family already has kids?
- What modifications are the dad and mom inclined to make to ease the child's transition?
- How do the parents feel about "open" adoption, that is, touch with the kid's start own family?
- How do the mother and father experience approximately welcoming a toddler from the foster care device or an orphanage who may additionally have experienced abuse or overlook?
- In instances of transracial or transcultural adoption—how do the mother and father feel approximately accommodating, assisting, and selling the child's nice cultural and racial identification?
- How will the parents tell family members and buddies, and how they will deal with

61

questions from family, pals, and strangers about adoption?

● How will the dad and mom answer their toddler's questions on adoption, the kid's historical past and records, birth circle of relatives, and the mother and father' reasons for adoption?

● How willing and in a position are they to are searching for assist for themselves or their baby while essential?

By answering the questions furnished above, one could be capable of objectively guide the family's decision-making process concerning the plan of adoption. Indeed, there are several elements that should be checked out and explored to see things in a bigger image. Adoption is a critical be counted that should be handled therefore. One cannot simply exchange his thoughts along the system for there are several events and emotions worried.

Handling the Process of Adoption

After going via the decision-making phase, every other stage that couples and households must undergo is the process of adoption itself. Unfortunately for prospective

62

dad and mom, the technique of adoption isn't just about signing papers and all. The technique is greater of a very burdensome and intrusive form of revel in for some.

The laws accompanying the adoption system vary throughout states. Depending on the form of adoption a pair is aiming at, additional laws might be relevant.

Among the first actual issue the couple should determine on in the method of adoption is the kind of adoption they may make. Are they going to consider inter-u . S . Or home adoption? Will they ask help from an adoption company? If yes, which one and the way to pick out? How are they going to cope with home take a look at questions? These are just a number of the initial worries that potential mother and father should be capable of deal with.

Also the manner of adoption takes time accordingly; couples should be capable of p.C. A bag of patience at the same time as going via the method. There are also planned factors and details that could delineate from the authentic plan of adoption. It is viable for a placement of the unique baby chosen or preferred, to take place anytime. Moreover, for the reason that procedure will make an effort, there are numerous possibilities for uncertain effects to show up. There are several opportunities, for example, the delivery parents all at once modified their minds concerning adoption or a relative all at once decided to take custody of the kid rather. Such events can show up and will preclude a pair's plan of adopting a child.

Prospective parents must additionally be prepared to submit necessities that commonly contain the following; evidence of income with tax return, evidence of health with clinical information, evidence of qualification with recommendation letters and evidence of marriage with a duplicate of marriage certificates. Different adoption organizations require varying documentations and different qualifications essential for the adoption. Some might require a evidence that as a minimum one of the couple would take day off from employment after receiving the child. Others would even require that adoptive parents don't have any biological baby. For couple with organic youngsters, a few agencies could have a maximum and minimal age range for their children as a requirement for eligibility for adoption.

The cost of adoption is any other count that have to be known for potential parents earlier the adoption process. Public adoption is most probable the most less costly kind, costing at least $2000; despite the fact that, extra often than not, kids to be had thru public agencies are generally young adults and children with severe disabilities. This organization is normally referred to as "tough-to-region" kids. Private adoptions generally fee between $10,000 and $12,000. The maximum high priced kind of adoption is the global one. To entire this adoption process, one wishes $20,000 to $35,000.

After the possible parents have completed the requirements for the adoption, they'll still await months or even a year earlier than they receive the kid. The waiting time differs for it largely relies upon at the availability of kids. Parents usually request for children with particular traits at some point of the procedure. The traits specific will make the ready time longer. For instance, a pair asked for a white toddler; the ready length will take so long as 18 months. A request for a black child, but, will just take one to 9 months. This fashion is often due to the fact there are greater black children available for adoption than white ones.

Adapting to Adoptive Parenting

Studies display that majority of the adoptive mother and father are happy with their decision. Nevertheless, some problems can nonetheless be experienced in the put up adoption length.

Post Adoption Depression Syndrome or PADS is the sensation of disappointment or being "let down" after months of looking ahead to parenthood. This, in line with researches, usually occurs inside a few weeks of the crowning glory of adoption. Becoming a figure isn't as smooth as how one imagines it. The weight of the obligations related to turning into actual dad and mom can be overwhelming for a few, specifically for first-time dad and mom. Creating an attachment with the kid might not be easy and from time to time several efforts fail, making the parent sense incapable of becoming an powerful dad or mum for the child.

For couples who undertake toddlers, it ought to be expected that there will be some sleepless nights, a number of diaper changing and other tiresome obligations that must be executed consequently and in a well timed manner. Most of the time, these parenting realities make a discern query his/her capability of becoming a parent for a child. There are going to be moments whilst parents might feel inadequate to deserve becoming a mom or a father to the followed baby.

Fortunately, dad and mom generally tend to triumph over the melancholy, as they adjust to the brand new existence. Nonetheless, if the melancholy endured for several weeks and is meddling with the productiveness and functioning of the parent worried, a expert help need to be sought.

Once a family determined on adopting a baby, they're as nicely selecting essential adjustments of their lifestyles. Everyone's function can have enormous modifications as soon as the child arrives home with his/her new parents. Most of the time, such modifications inside the position, regardless of how subtle it's far, could make a person sense different in a single way or any other. The couple is now a mother and a father. The followed baby is now a part of a brand new own family. If the couple has a organic son/daughter, then his/her function will trade right into a brother or a sister. Adjusting to the brand new roles is the part this is by no means smooth. The arrival of the followed infant might appear to push via drastic changes in the family.

Attachments and love are the common emotional grounds that appear to be difficult to set up within the new own family putting. Some adopted children may have the sensation of alienation within the new own family gadget. For the parents, connecting with the child and making him/her sense "at home" may be tough. Some dad and mom can effortlessly be disheartened by means of seeing their efforts to create a bond produce too little or no impact in any respect. Some mother and father are troubled with the way to start establishing connections with the kid.

Establishing the Connection

What bothers maximum adoptive dad and mom is the feeling that no kind of bond or connection appears to glide evidently even though the adopted baby is residing with the circle of relatives already. The hassle now and again is that parents want end result too fast. They must understand that the child wishes time to modify with the most important

68

adjustments in his/her existence. Moreover, how lengthy would the adjustment period is cannot be foretold for it will largely rely on the child's way of coping and adjusting. Therefore, parents must deliver the child the time he/she wishes, but at the identical time they have to no longer halt efforts in trying to reveal love and affection, after all of the kid is theirs now.

If connection does not are available naturally, then establish it. One way for mother and father to assist the system of building a relationship with the adopted child is through engaging the kid in all circle of relatives sports. Creating a own family ritual would be of outstanding help. The infant have to experience concerned with the whole lot the family is worried of, so he/she will be able to gradually be removed from the prison of alienation.

Making the kid feel vital is likewise pivotal. An adopted toddler would possibly have horrific reports with her organic circle of relatives; for that reason letting her recognise and feel that her new own family is a lot specific in an awesome way may inspire her to fulfill the mother and father' efforts half-way with her own.

Creating a family photograph book could additionally help the child experience included inside the circle of relatives. Once a baby sees that her snap shots are blanketed inside the own family e-book, then she will have the feeling of belongingness. Take pictures of the whole own family and placed them in frames to be displayed across the residence. This can even help the child modify in his/her new circle of relatives placing easier.

Another way is the very fundamental technique of mastering the kid individually. Primarily, the adoption organisation have to have given valuable statistics about the child and his/her background. Nonetheless, understanding the child personally will make dad and mom extra connected to the kid, and vice versa. Establishing a dating always starts offevolved from the getting-to-recognize degree; dad and mom ought to do that to achieve the preferred form of dating with the followed child. Parents need to find time to speak with the kid. At first, this could now not be clean for the mother and father would possibly receive silence for answers. Nonetheless, this isn't a purpose to surrender;

it's miles actually a cause to continue. An unfaltering attempt can pay.

Knowing any other couple that followed a child 2 to 10 years in the past can be useful within the technique. Sharing stories with them would possibly deliver encouragements and new views to new mother and father. Learning from their tales of changes will deliver parents new techniques to try. Nonetheless, mother and father have to maintain in thoughts that everyone is particular and so are situations. Hence, one need to no longer count on that each method or approach that worked for one family will paintings for his/her own.

Lastly, dad and mom need to be organized with solutions. The baby will surely ask matters he/she cannot recognize. By that time, one have to be able to have pleasurable solutions. In addition to this, other human beings will genuinely ask several questions; as a result, one must have solutions readily to be had.

If parents assume that the child's adjustment is taking goodbye or their personal adjustment is, then they must help the adjustment system itself. Adjustment is a technique; mother and father have to give it

71

the time important at the same time as nourishing regions like love, affection and care which can be pivotal to the establishment of a sturdy bond and courting with the adopted toddler.

Adoption: Looking at Both Sides of the Coin

There are numerous troubles concerning adoption and among the maximum debatable consists of open adoption and transracial adoption. Whether those sorts of adoption are right or mistaken, helpful or adverse is still debated until now. This a part of the e book will gift both facets of the coin starting with open adoption.

Open adoption, as discussed in advance, is a kind of adoption whereby adoptive parents and delivery dad and mom percentage records and contacts before, throughout or even after the system of adoption has been finished.

Pros and Cons of Open Adoption for the Adopted Person

The benefits of open adoption involve the advent of an more suitable sense of self by the adopted character. With the traditional

72

closed adoption, the organization will not expose any information approximately the child's biological parents. Thus, nothing can be recognized approximately the child's biological origins. The motive why open adoption is supported by means of most experts in this area is due to the alarming instances of heightened identification confusion displayed via followed youngsters. With open adoption, the kid may be fully informed of his/her full history.

Open adoption will permit the character adopted to know his/her self holistically. Accurate data about the followed individual's cultural and ethnic historical past will be won from open adoption. Moreover, correct medical records may be possessed. This is very vital to completely check the followed individual, medically talking. In case he/she develops certain infection in existence, a whole and precise clinical records might be of awesome help in finding appropriate treatment and/or medicine.

The followed person will also be free of any emotional impact resulting from understanding nothing about his own starting place. It is very common for an followed character to sense "incomplete" as soon as he has learned approximately his adoption. Regardless if the adoptive mother and father have been capable of offer enough love, care and affection to the adopted son, he will still suffer some emotional problem due to the notion that the majority of who he's stays unknown.

Open adoption will even take away any misconceptions the adopted character would possibly increase because of the secrecy of the identification of his/her actual parents. It is also much more likely that the man or woman adopted will take the situation in a greater mature way. Open adoption gets rid of haunting questions; accordingly, saving the individual from the hassle of walking away.

Indeed there are sizeable benefits of open adoption for the individual adopted. Nonetheless, there are also drawbacks with this type of openness.

With open adoption, the adoptee can get admission to the information of his/her biological dad and mom and may pursue meeting them. Also, the individual can opt no longer to peer or know them in my opinion. When the previous is selected with the aid of the kid, it can not be avoided for the adoptive dad and mom to be harm. If the adoptee

74

desires to keep away from hurting them, however is emotionally bothered with the aid of the sensation of incompleteness, then he have to recognise that open adoption can cause more emotional uncertainty than closed adoption. Sometimes understanding greater brings complication in place of solution.

Another downside of open adoption is the perception that the child is unwanted by his/her biological dad and mom. It is an inevitable notion specially for the followed individual. This concept can trigger hatred to organic dad and mom and even to oneself. For someone to recognise that he turned into given away with the aid of his own parents will truely stir negative principles about oneself.

Pros and Cons of Open Adoption for the Birth Parents

Open Adoption can provide several advantages for the organic dad and mom, as properly. Perhaps, not anything is greater important for a delivery parent than to know that his/her toddler is in proper palms. With open adoption, birth dad and mom will understand the sort of own family who will raise his/her baby. This will ease the tension and worry that the delivery mother and father are experiencing. In addition, the grieving technique will no longer be very hard for the biological parents if they are properly-informed of the kid's wherein-approximately.

Open adoption may even open possibilities for the birth parents to speak about the problem of adoption with the kid. With closed adoption, there is no manner for the organic dad and mom to give an explanation for to the followed individual why he/she changed into given up for adoption.

The biological mother and father may even have the risk to nevertheless be involved with the child's existence. Provided that this type of setting is agreed upon by using the adoptive mother and father, delivery parents want not be strangers for the adopted character.

Open adoption, however, also can put up disadvantages for the biological mother and father. Emotions are simply so sturdy at instances that although beginning mother and father were able to offer the purpose for adoption together with different answers to the adopted person's questions; the adoptee will nonetheless resent him. Hatred directly

76

addressed to a birth mother/father can be very painful.

With open adoption, other humans not at once concerned with the adoption be counted can vicinity judgments upon the start parents. In a conservative social context, buddies might connect stigma to the beginning parents for sending their toddler for adoption. A stigma is by no means an smooth rely that someone may be over with after a brief at the same time as. Negative notions approximately them positioned by way of the judging eyes of the community will honestly purpose emotional troubles for the biological parents. This is exactly what closed adoption is warding off. Secrecy somehow can guard start mother and father from unwanted judgments and unsolicited opinion coming from different humans, who, most likely, have the least knowledge of the situation.

Pros and Cons of Open Adoption for the Adoptive Parents

Some of the blessings of open adoption for the adoptive dad and mom encompass the potential to be concerned in pre-birth medical doctor's visits until delivery. This permits adoptive dad and mom to be assured that the beginning mom is in top and wholesome condition during being pregnant. If they can assist the biological mother with the pregnancy and in a while shipping of the kid, then a strong feeling of reference to the child prior to his birth can be set up via the adoptive dad and mom. With this, building connections with the non-biological baby afterward will no longer be that hard.

The openness of statistics in adoption may also permit adoptive dad and mom to remove the concern of the unknown. This, possibly, is the most promising benefit of open adoption. Among the fears that adoptive mother and father may have include the possibility that at some point, the child's organic parents will come knocking on their door to get the him/her.

The negative aspects of open adoption for the adoptive dad and mom may include the fear and possibility that the followed baby will choose his/her organic dad and mom over them. Adoptive dad and mom will usually have such problem; that notwithstanding their efforts to grow to be the nice parents they could in all likelihood be for the child, blood might be truely thicker than water.

Role confusion also can be stirred by way of open adoption. Having a child with two moms and fathers is a difficult circle of relatives set-up. The ambiguity of wherein a figure's (biological and non-organic) responsibility starts offevolved and ends can function a drawback in making this complicated own family device paintings.

These are simply a number of the pros and cons of adopting a infant through an open adoption. The lives of all of the parties worried in such sort of adoption might be more complex in real normal experiences than how they appear in texts. Adopting a infant is certainly a main decision with fine and bad impact that have to be dealt with for a totally lengthy time period, possibly even a lifetime.

Transracial Adoption: Pros and Cons

Another essential problem in the adoption area involves transracial adoption. This refers to some adopting a baby who belongs to a exclusive cultural historical past. Whether this sort of adoption is beneficial or especially disruptive is a primary debate that runs till now.

The Cons

One most important claim that opponents of transracial adoption country is that a white own family adopting a black child can damage the child within the technique. According to warring parties, simplest parents belonging to the equal racial origin can offer an powerful parenting to the kid. For instance, simplest black mother and father can educate a black infant the right way of handling racism. This is in general because they, as blacks, maximum probably have experienced coping with such. According to combatants, a white family can't cope with this critical thing correctly especially because they lack any enjoy related to the issue of racism. As said by means of critics of transracial adoption, for a child to meet the correct mental improvement, he/she should be located with dad and mom of the identical cultural orientation.

Another claim is that adoptive parents are also harmed within the method of transracial adoption. White mother and father will probable be subjected to intrusiveness, hostility and/or prejudice for adopting transracially. For example, humans surrounding a white couple will now not effortlessly get used to the truth that they followed a black child. Interviews carried out to white dad and mom screen that they receive intrusive questions from instantaneous family and pals simply due to transracial adoption. The physical distinction on my own might make different humans marvel about the scenario. In addition to this, parents who followed transracially commonly receive "the appearance" or "the stare" from other people this is very a lot unpleasant.

On the alternative hand, supporters of transracial adoption maintain that this kind of adoption gives precise blessings for the children. A permanent and healthful domestic is what a baby needs. Racial matching ought to not be the priority mainly if it is able to cause put off to the possibility for a child to have a family.

The dating between the adoptive parents and the kid is likewise deemed deeper and more potent frequently due to the fact the bond changed into no longer compelled by using biological-relatedness alternatively it become built absolutely from the foundation of the bond itself.

The obvious bodily differences will even function reminders for mother and father that the kid is followed. The suitable aspect approximately this is that mother and father may have extra reasons to simply accept the kid as he/she is; as a consequence, heading off placing unreasonable expectancies of likeness in abilties and personalities delivered by using false organic dating.

In addition to this, individuals who adopt transracially display an admirable trait which makes them the maximum qualified individuals to adopt. If a pair does no longer examine race as an critical component in adoption, then they see no distinction amongst children belonging to distinctive cultural heritages. They are dad and mom who're commonly properly knowledgeable about treating all and sundry similarly. Moreover, mother and father who favor to adopt transracially are displaying excessive-levels of dedication in the technique of adoption.

Among the "stranger" adoption kinds, transracial adoption posts the most venture. Parents contain in such adoption have to have to address cultural differences aside from biological un-relatedness. By adopting a baby from unique race, dad and mom display more dedication for notwithstanding the attention that this sort of adoption is the most tough of all, they nevertheless pursue the technique.

Transracial adoption also can gain the society itself. Having families, composed of mother and father and youngsters from exceptional cultural historical past, round will lessen societal racism and racial anxiety. Witnessing that human beings from distinctive race can come to be one and united as a own family will make humans understand that the colour of the pores and skin isn't an important aspect of the human existence.

Parents who adopt transracially can also offer a new attitude to the society whose theory of a own family and race stays traditional. Parents who followed kids from extraordinary race are racially open-minded even earlier than receiving the child. Moreover, these parents found out via interviews that they have become extra accepting to others after adopting transracially.

Prejudice is maximum probable attributed to the shortage of social contact. People feel one-of-a-kind from one another because there may be no ground that might let them know each other in a deeper manner. Having households with followed youngsters from unique cultural history may be an excellent begin to get rid of prejudice and racism inside the entire society.

Chapter 6: Why Tell Your Child The Truth

Normally for children raised by their biological mother and father, records about themselves aren't kept and are some thing recognised ever because they could handle comprehension. But for kids who are raised and cared for by adoptive dad and mom, understanding who they truly are is a necessity and a probably existence-converting occasion. For the parents who cared and loved those kids even supposing they're now not biologically associated, letting the tale of adoption slip from their mouth is something that can be dreadful, tough, and painful. Some, due to worry of what might also manifest, might even determine they could in no way inform their kids they're adopted. But to be able to only occur in a determine's thoughts if she does not know what to do, when to do it, and the way to prepare her child approximately these things.

Keeping your infant's adoption tale from him is essentially stealing part of his identification. It will only cause something irreparable—it might ruin down your dating with him. You cannot prevent him from thinking why he

85

seems exclusive—specifically while he gets older. And worse, there may be a first rate risk he will research from someone else that he is adopted. He would feel betrayed and speculate about the reasons he became left through his organic dad and mom. It could be a lot tougher for both of you.

Furthermore, for adopted transracial kids, the boom in their hobby approximately their being different is something unavoidable. Hence, it might be clever to begin the procedure of telling the story of his adoption as soon as he reaches the age whilst he can already realize things.

Every toddler deserves to recognize who they in reality are. Having complete know-how approximately oneself greatly will increase shallowness and self confidence. Everyone really desires to learn their beyond in order for them to look forward to and build their destiny.

Prepare Yourself

Before we move right down to the glide of the process, it's miles essential with a purpose to be equipped. The surprise and ache you could sense may be equal to what your baby might also enjoy while he's advised about his adoption. Though you may most effective wager what would happen when your baby eventually recognize that he is adopted—whether it'll grow to be clean for each of you or not—if you prepare your self for the worst, desire for the first-rate, and accept regardless of the final results may be, matters could be less complicated for you.

Below is a approach that let you equipped your self. Every step right here incorporates "what to anticipate" and "what to wish" components in addition to explanation to returned it up.

What to anticipate
Expect your toddler to be greatly surprised and depressed whilst he eventually hears that he's adopted.

What to wish
Hope that after something he felt, or but shocked he's, he will still evenly and peacefully receive that he's followed.
Your toddler can infrequently manage distressing situations like this. Give him time

and area to understand matters properly and allow him think matters over.

What to assume
Expect that he can be mad at you due to preserving the story of adoption from him.

What to pray
Hope that through the years, he will understand that you do now not need to be his birth figure for the 2 of you to have a real parent-child dating.
Your child might also feel betrayed due to the fact you stored the reality from him for a time. This is herbal. But after some time, he will workout that he is cherished and there is no cause for him to be furious at you.

What to anticipate
Expect him to experience he is worthless, deserted, and incomplete.

What to pray
Hope that he's going to soon see that it isn't due to him however because of his delivery dad and mom that he was given up for adoption.

It is natural for a child to experience that the reason he was given away is because there's some thing incorrect with him. But because of the exceptional love you have got proven and are displaying him, he's going to realize how perfect he is for your eyes.

What to count on
Your courting with him will by no means be as good because it turned into earlier than you instructed him about the adoption.

What to pray
Hope that as time passes, your toddler will understand how an awful lot you adore him.
Upon understanding he's adopted, he may experience a touch aware being with you due to the fact he can also still have the choice to know who his birth parents are and why they gave him up for adoption. But that choice—finished or not—will not stop your baby from longing for your love.

What to anticipate
Your baby will start to think which you love your beginning children greater than him.

What to pray

Hope that with the effort you exert to hold your courting with him at par with what you've got together with your organic children, he's going to understand that you love all your kids – which include him - equally.

It is natural for him to think of that. Hence, it's miles vital that you in no way skimp on the love and attention you supply your child. Nothing have to exchange. Show him that he is your child no matter what.

The Process of Telling

Telling your child about the adoption is a lifelong technique. Time is an vital element here. It is important which you plan about this even before adopting, and set it in motion whilst he's still younger. It does no longer necessarily suggest you ought to inform him right away that he is adopted. But there are small steps that you could take. Every step ought to be in step with his highbrow and emotional adulthood stage. The technique begins with shaping his view of adoption. If a infant does now not have a advantageous view on it, it is going to be tougher for him to accept the fact that he is followed.

Ages 1-5

Children inside this age bracket suppose the arena revolves around them. They suppose actually and one-dimensionally. Their brains start to burst with questions concerning things that seem alien to them—including adoption and pregnancy. So it's miles pretty crucial to know the way to react properly on their queries.

Your baby's interest is your signal so that you can start the reason. But if you don't see it coming, you may go in advance and discuss the stated topics with him.

Explaining Pregnancy to Your Child

In order in your baby to discover adoption from being pregnant, tell him the motive of being pregnant from a juvenile attitude. It is likewise very crucial to consciousness on the start method and ensure to contain your baby in your rationalization.

Here's a sample clarification:

"Harry, pregnancy is the process of maintaining a infant inner his mommy's tummy due to the fact his parents love him and they want him to stay in this world with them. Mothers supply beginning to their

91

children due to the fact having a child is the fine feeling a discern could have."

Explaining Adoption

In order for him to have an awesome know-how of adoption, explain it too in a way he can recognize.

For instance, your tale can pass like this:

"Harry, adoption occurs because a person simply desires to have and love a toddler."

Explaining That Adoption is Equal to the Birth Process

For him to absolutely draw close adoption as a completely appropriate component, provide an explanation for that adoption and the start system are similar.

Your tale need to go like this:

"Harry, it is not vital how parents have their toddler. What is essential is that they love him. Adoption and giving birth are both good ways of getting a baby. Some youngsters are fortunate they had been each born and adopted."

Explaining Why He or She is Different

If your toddler is exclusive in race, or totally awesome in physical features, he will effortlessly become aware about his being unique from you. But at this age bracket, he desires guarantee that he is your baby and also you ought to prevent him from feeling he's an outcast. It doesn't necessarily mean you need to reveal the statistics about his delivery mother and father proper away. Explain it to him in a manner that he can recognize and accept.

If your toddler asks why he's distinctive, you can phrase your answer this manner:

"Harry, we is probably a little distinctive in phrases of the color of our pores and skin or eyes or hair, but don't forget that we like you. People are one of a kind from one another. It's just like how books want distinct titles so we don't get harassed. See, no person is identical. And your forte will no longer stop me from loving you."

In order to your toddler to have a fantastic view of adoption, it is probably wise to tell him or her bedtime testimonies that consist of adopted characters. Or watch films with him that consist of characters who are followed. Choose the ones in an effort to assist him draw close adoption whole-heartedly.

Also, keep in mind that this isn't a one-shot procedure. The pointers above must be achieved consistently and whenever vital.

For a Child among the Ages 6 and 9

Your baby, within this age duration, already has a broader information of the distinctive ways of getting a toddler. He already has a clean attitude on adoption. And most significantly, you and your child likely have already set up a near and heat relationship. This is the time that he's closest to you; therefore, telling him about his adoption at this level can reduce the emotional impact this information may have on him.

When telling his adoption story, keep away from being rely-of-school if the records regarding his dad and mom are some thing his innocence cannot yet take or something that can make him upset approximately his parents in addition to himself. For example, you wouldn't inform to your baby his mom gave start to him when she was 17, or that her mother turned into an alcoholic. What you need to tell him instead is that his start dad and mom love him and they need him to have a better future that's why he changed into put up for adoption.

After telling your baby, he'll start to feel abandoned or left out. He will start to speculate approximately the motives he became "given away". Children deal with this depressing time of their own way. Some brazenly speak approximately it; some are reclusive and pretend their feelings; a few are agitated approximately it; and some do not care about their adoption story. The excellent you may do is to provide your shoulder to him. Ask your infant how he feels and try to recognize it.

For a Child Between the Ages 9 and 11
Keeping your baby's advantageous view about adoption does now not forestall at any age duration. Though you're carried out with explaining the distinction of being pregnant and the birth technique from adoption, speakme about the instances surrounding his delivery is essential. At this age period, your toddler will sporadically enjoy excessive feelings of loss, grief, incompleteness, and a yearning for his birth parents – their identification as well as their present whereabouts.
Some of the questions that can be nagging your child are the subsequent:

95

- Do my beginning parents love me?
- If they love me, why did they depart me?
- So many unmarried-parents live thankfully with their infant, why turned into my mom no longer able to do the equal with me?
- Couldn't my mother and father have sacrificed for me?
- Where are they now?
- How are they now?
- Do my adoptive parents love me?

Your baby might also experience a little hatred in the direction of his birth dad and mom due to the fact it's far nonetheless hard for him to accept the fact that he's adopted. At the same time, he may also doubt the love you're displaying him. What you need to do is to hold an ongoing and open talk with him. Remember that this ordeal is a challenge both the adoptive dad and mom and the child need to face.

Regarding how the ones questions need to be answered, at this age duration, uncovering statistics which could nonetheless make him sense disillusioned about his fate and that of his mother and father isn't but appropriate. Telling lifestyles's various gloomy occasions continues to be past his knowledge and emotional coverage. What you must do as a substitute is to protect his delivery dad and mom. Diminish the hatred he is feeling towards his delivery mother and father by means of assuring him that they love him, and then turn the highlight on you . For instance, whilst answering the query:

"So many unmarried-mother and father stay fortunately with their baby, why become my mom now not capable of do the same with me?"

Do no longer offer a reaction with the intention to supply your toddler a bad view of his mother and father. Your solution must be some thing like this:

"Harry, I recognise it's far tough for you. It is tough for me too. But it's far an awful lot tougher for your start mother and father. This is because in order with a purpose to have a better lifestyles, they gave up the chance to elevate you. Harry, your dad and mom should be so courageous to face every day without you by using their aspect."

Letting your toddler construct a high quality photo of his beginning mother and father right now will make it simpler for him to digest the fact when he's older.

97

Forming Your Child's Identity

Adolescence is that part of someone's life wherein he tries to form his identification some distance from the world he knew at domestic. Discovering his capabilities, exploring different things, reaching for his dreams... This is a essential segment for him, and a lot greater essential for an adopted infant if the statistics approximately his delivery dad and mom and approximately himself is missing. You without a doubt should tell him the truth at this factor. Furthermore, as they grow antique, adopted kids will discover it tough to in shape within the international they're in; that is specifically proper for trans racial adopted children. Your toddler can also feel and spot that he's distinctive when he's at home, given the fact that his skin shade is distinct from anybody inside the circle of relatives. Details approximately their start dad and mom and about their adoption tale are the key for them to completely apprehend who they are and why they appear so one-of-a-kind. As dad and mom, you wouldn't need your baby to suffer underneath the curse of adoption.

Children who are 12-18 years antique have already got the capability and adulthood to just accept how adoption changed their fate. Their highbrow and emotional maturity has already grown through leaps and limits at those ages. Your infant can now comprehend the truth that his mother is an alcoholic, or his mom become pregnant at 17, or died giving birth to him. Furthermore, it will be less difficult for him to understand that there's a purpose you didn't expose these records to him earlier than.

As your baby enters this tough part of his lifestyles, his demands to recognise extra about himself, about his beginning dad and mom, and the circumstances that surrounded his adoption tale could be stronger. He will now realise that the story of adoption you have got provided earlier to him is insufficient. He will start to crave for more actual, deeper, and distinctive answers. Your toddler may even begin to suppose of different motives simply to fill the void you created. But his interest can lead him to confusion. His questions will start to contain not only his start mother and father but additionally himself. "What turned into incorrect with me? Can't they love me? Didn't they want to have a toddler?"

It is your responsibility, as an adoptive determine, to preserve your infant from questioning he's a mistake and/or a failure, or that he doesn't need to be cherished.

During this age duration, these are the troubles that need to be discussed with him:

Facts About The Birth parents

As your child blooms right into a youngster, his longing for the records about his beginning parents will become inevitable. And at this time, there is no point to continue to inform your baby the adoption tale you made up whilst he became more youthful. He would need the info and the fact from you. As your teenage toddler grows older, he'd want to have a far deeper information of his delivery dad and mom. He'd need to sense complete. Though the statistics about your child's beginning mother and father are potentially provoking or harmful, leaving him fantasizing approximately the purpose they left him may be tons greater antagonizing. Generally, truth is favored.

Reason He turned into Adopted

Why did you undertake your infant? Was it that he turned into left at your front door? Or was he passed to you by someone you didn't recognize? Whatever the information surrounding his adoption, he merits to understand them. Truth be told, there may be no cause if you want to maintain his adoption tale from him. Just like when you informed him that he is adopted, it'd be hard at the beginning. But over time, he'll learn how to be given what befell to him.

The Birth mother and father' Condition
Your toddler, even though he feels hatred towards his beginning dad and mom, won't stop considering the present circumstance of his birth mother and father. These may be amongst his questions: How are they now? Is my mother nevertheless alive? Do I have siblings? Are they k?
Provide data approximately his organic family if you can. Not understanding the data will push your infant to think bad thoughts about his delivery mother and father' present circumstance. Though the fact approximately their circumstance can disenchanted or fear him, thinking some thing terrible that isn't sincerely taking place is doubtlessly extra negative. Knowing the facts—although these

101

are hard to simply accept—is a remedy for your infant.

Reason He Was Given Up for Adoption
"Was there anything incorrect with me?" "Didn't they love me?" "Was I now not really worth loving?" Your baby will also be unique these questions.

It is crucial for your baby to understand the cause he become placed up for adoption and/or left by means of his mother and father. He desires to make feel of the complete tale of his adoption.

How to Address Your Child's Feelings

There's no telling how lengthy the emotional turmoil your toddler's story of adoption can bring him will ultimate. It tremendously relies upon on the way you contain yourself and the way you deal with his feelings. Even even though it is clear your toddler has subsequently universal that he changed into followed, he may also still sense doubtful approximately sure things. He would possibly ask those: Do my adoptive mother and father love me like they love their delivery children?

Do they remorse of adopting me? Do I deserve their love?

It is normal for him to feel this way. But leaving your child to lick his wounds just like with a view to not, in any manner, do away with the questions going on inner his mind. You want to keep an awesome courting with him. This chapter will inform you a way to keep your courting together with your baby as proper as it changed into.

Talk to Your Child About School
During meal instances or whilst there is a danger, attempt to ask him how his college-existence goes. It is an guarantee that you care about his achievements or screw ups; which you care about him.

Acknowledge His or Her Achievements
Your toddler were given an A+. How need to you react? Well, this tip have to observe to all mom-and-child relationships, which include that between you and your followed baby. You have to sincerely apprehend all the good stuff he does—whether these are small or huge achievements.

Avoid Getting Infuriated When Your Child Fails

Getting indignant at him because of his failures (huge or small) can exacerbate his negative emotions towards himself, you, and his organic dad and mom. Though of route being indignant at instances is unmanageable, and once in a while wished, choose the times whilst you need to set free your anger. Know whilst anger is not certainly wished. Control it if possible.

Bond with Your Child

Your time collectively must now not lessen nor trade just because some thing approximately your child is unveiled. Continue doing your bonding sports, whether or not it's looking your favored TV show collectively, or visiting your favorite theme park. Besides, that is the perfect time for you to reveal that your love for him has not modified.

Attend Your Child's School Activities

Attending college sports, mainly people who require mother and father to move will make him experience he is important to you. Give him the aid he needs with faculty initiatives and different campus activities.

Ask How He or She Feels About Adoption
This step will observe for your toddler if he's 6-18 years old. Talking to him approximately his adoption tale can absolutely ease the pain he keeps internal. Show him that it's miles k that he is adopted. You need to guarantee him that his adoption story doesn't make him different out of your other children. Ask your infant what he feels approximately it, and reply in a positive manner.

The most critical step in assisting your child get via this miserable time is maintaining all lines of communique open. You must change mind. And you ought to always recognize him.

Remember that each one the steps given in this book ought to now not be performed out of guilt or because you sense compelled to do so. Also, the suggestions given are clearly instinctive to mother and father of followed youngsters who actually love and care for their baby. Maintaining an excellent relationship together with your child—followed or no longer—is not a need but a responsibility. You love your baby because you love him. There should be no different reason for this.

Chapter 7: Preparing To Adopt

There are many motives why humans want to adopt. In this ebook, we can best remember non-relative adoptions, or adoptions involving a toddler who isn't biologically related to the potential dad and mom. The fundamental reasons people undertake include:

1. The couple cannot have a biological child in their very own. This is undoubtedly the maximum commonplace reason why couples prefer to undertake. The couple can be infertile or there can be a scientific purpose that makes it hazardous for the mother to grow to be pregnant and carry a baby to term.

2. They are a same-sex couple who would love to begin a family. This is becoming an increasingly more famous reason for adoption given the growing recognition by using society of equal sex unions.

three. The couple may also select to undertake in preference to having a organic toddler in their own. In this case, the couple might also experience that it is greater critical to help an orphan who has no own family instead of conceiving considered one of their own. However, this does not suggest that the couple will not pick to have a biological child later, as seen inside the case of Angelina Jolie, who followed Maddox and Zahara before she and partner Brad Pitt had their own biological infant.

Once you have made the choice to undertake based totally to your own personal motives for doing so, you need to decide type of adoption you want to pursue – adopting a child domestically or from distant places. Here are a number of the inquiries to preserve in mind when making this important choice:

1.   How old is the kid you want to adopt? If you're snug with adopting an older child or a infant, you can adopt a baby from everywhere; if you need a new child, but, your simplest option is to adopt from america. Angelina Jolie, for instance, followed three yr old Pax from Vietnam.

2.   Do you need get admission to to the social and scientific records of the delivery households? In a home adoption, this facts is simply available, at the same time as if you adopt from overseas, it might be extra difficult to acquire.

3.   How quickly do you need the adoption to be completed? In each worldwide and home

adoptions, there is in reality no way to inform when the adoption may be completed, although with nearby adoptions, you have got a touch more control over the timeframe of the process. However, worldwide adoptions can be a bit extra predictable, although factors including political unrest can effect how lengthy it takes to finish an adoption.

four.   Do you need to preserve contact with the delivery mother? Most adoptive dad and mom select an global adoption due to the fact they need to absolutely cut off touch with the birth own family. On the opposite hand, with many home adoptions, at least, the delivery mom is aware of the primary names of the adoptive parents. Often, the start mother and father and the adoptive dad and mom may additionally meet or have talked at the telephone as a manner to guarantee them that the child is going to an amazing home. The start mom may even receive images and different updates on how the child is doing, which are forwarded from the adoption agency. These updates are meant as a manner to ease the delivery mother's mind that she made the right choice in giving upthe child for adoption as she can see that they're dwelling in an amazing home, with loving mother and father.

five.   How a great deal can you manage to pay for to spend on the adoption? Realistically, you should expect to spend at the least $20,000 whether or not you undertake locally or from overseas. However, with worldwide adoptions, the fees have a tendency to be more predictable because they're already fixed, even as in domestic adoptions, sudden costs may additionally crop up, inclusive of health expenses for the delivery mom.

One closing aspect to speak approximately is a few adoptive mother and father' worries over the start mother unexpectedly expressing regret and then seeking to get her child back. In reality, this rarely happens as maximum delivery moms have idea over their selection and frequent it absolutely. In addition, even in a so-known as semi-open adoption, the beginning mom does no longer have any contact info for the adoptive parents, and for that reason, has no way to attain them. Even if she may want to locate the adoptive parents, once she gave the kid up for adoption, she no longer has any criminal rights over her or him.

Preparing to Be an Adoptive Parent

Before making a decision about adoption, you must talk it first with your kids, if you have any. You must get yourself up to speed with how your children experience approximately adopting a new brother or sister. In addition, you should also deliver other contributors of your instantaneous and prolonged circle of relatives into the discussions because they may ultimately play their very own element in assisting increase the kid.

Apart from joint family discussions, you could need to keep man or woman discussions with precise family members for the reason that they will be uncomfortable with expressing their reviews in such an open setting. Make sure which you guarantee them that something they feel is k and that their evaluations could be respected and brought into account inside the selection-making manner.

If circle of relatives participants have any concerns, you need to make certain to renowned them and don't allow yourself to feel threatened. Address those concerns squarely and in a non-adversarial manner. Stress how the adoption contributes to your

111

lengthy-time period dreams in your circle of relatives.

The Adoption Process

Once you've decided what form of adoption you need to pursue, you can start the adoption process. However, before you initiate the adoption system, you have to look up the laws on your country concerning adoption for the reason that this could prevent lots of trouble later. In particular, right here are a number of the matters you need to look at:

1.   How soon after giving delivery can the organic mom and/or father provide consent for an adoption?

2.   How long after signing the adoption agreement does it end up irrevocable? Is the toddler mechanically again to the delivery mom once the consent is revoked?

3.   What fees can the birth dad and mom fee to the adoptive dad and mom and over what time period?

four.   Are you allowed to promote it for birth parents?

You can discover extra distinct records on legal guidelines on adoption of your country at the net Child Welfare Information Gateway of the United States Department of Health and Human Services.

Eligibility to Adopt

Generally, a couple or single character can be eligible to undertake with no other conditions connected in 13 states and the District of Columbia. However, man or woman states can also have other eligibility necessities relying on their neighborhood legal guidelines. For example, age requirements range, with six states requiring potential mother and father to be as a minimum eighteen and six other states requiring that the dad and mom be at least ten years older than the adoptive infant. The majority of states also require that adoptive dad and mom be residents of the country where the adoption is being performed although some others allow out-of-state adoptions. The question of gay and lesbian couples adopting is also difficult in some states, with Florida, as an instance, specifically prohibiting it even as Utah prohibits adoptions by means of couples who aren't legally married, which may be interpreted as protecting gay couples.

While all states permit youngsters to be adopted, 3 states specify that the kid ought to

113

be under eighteen. In addition, twenty five states permit adults to be adopted via no longer specifying an age requirement for the prospective adoptee. Alabama and Ohio allow the adoption of adults if they're permanently bodily disabled or mentally retarded.

In addition, all potential dad and mom need to go through a family or home examine, for you to now not simplest train them on the adoption method and better prepare them for welcoming a brand new infant into their home but additionally compare their fitness to undertake and gather sufficient facts to help the social employee evaluate which child could be best served by using being placed with this particular own family.

The Domestic Adoption Process

To start the adoption process, pick out which adoption professional or employer you need to paintings with. Which one you choose relies upon at the sort of toddler which you want to undertake. Your options encompass:

1.   Public enterprise adoption. These companies mainly deal with the adoption of children who are within the foster care device. These kids are in the machine because they had been taken far from their households for numerous motives inclusive of

114

abuse or forget about. If you are open to adopting older youngsters, those of shade, people with disabilities or siblings, then you can do not forget adopting thru a public agency. However, you and your family have to be prepared to cope with the unique wishes these children may additionally have; as an instance, many are traumatized because of abuse and may require counseling. To qualify for adopting a baby from foster care, you don't need to own your private home, be married or earn a sure income so long as your social employee determines that you are strong and mature and able to provide the child with a very good home.

2. Licensed private organization. The requirements for adopting a infant from a non-public company are more stringent than those from public ones, in particular in case you want to undertake an little one. Birth mothers relinquish their parental rights to the employer, which then reveals adoptive parents for the kid. Waiting instances for adoption range relying on when the delivery parent selects a couple as prospective applicants to undertake their toddler. In addition, sure corporations may also restriction the candidates to individuals who

115

in shape sure criteria, including the ones belonging to a selected religious association or who're married.

three. Independent adoption. In this sort of adoption, the adoptive family enters into an settlement with a pregnant mom or expectant dad and mom to adopt their toddler after giving delivery, and an legal professional facilitates them with the prison a part of the procedure. Once the mother gives delivery on the sanatorium, the infant is usually already given to the adoptive parents. To formalize the adoption agreement, the start mother usually provides a written consent which must be authorized through the courts. Not all states permit impartial adoptions so that you need to test your nearby laws to peer if you can undertake through this channel.

4. Unlicensed paid facilitators. These facilitators connect prospective parents with expectant couples for a charge; but, due to the fact they paintings outside of any prison channels, there's a extraordinarily high danger that the adoption will now not exercise session and the possible parents haven't any recourse under the regulation. Many states also limit this practice so that

you ought to take a look at your neighborhood legal guidelines first earlier than the use of the services of a facilitator.

The International Adoption Process

The requirements for adopting a infant from some other u . S . A . Vary depending on their specific legal guidelines; in standard, however, a pair trying to undertake are placed on a ready listing and they may be matched to kids who turn out to be to be had for adoption. The potential parents are furnished with whatever own family history or medical history the child has to be had for you to make the choice whether or not or now not to undertake, even though in lots of instances, the statistics to be had can be skimpy. In this case, the couple may additionally want to discuss with a pediatrician who makes a speciality of decoding inter-u . S . Adoption referral statistics. The parents can also want to journey to the u . S . A . Wherein the kid is from to be able to pick out them up, and some countries may also require that the dad and mom make a couple of experience earlier than they could take the kid again with them.

If you are adopting a toddler from a rustic this is signatory to the Hague Convention on the

Protection of Children and Cooperation in Respect of Inter-country Adoption, there are positive mandated requirements that potential mother and father ought to comply with. These include running with an accredited or accredited issuer who makes a speciality of Hague Convention adoption offerings, having a home examine completed and finishing at the least ten hours of mandated permitted training. The baby should also fit the definition of adoptee below the guidelines of the Convention and be eligible for adoption beneath the laws of their u . S . A . Of origin. For adoptions from a non-Hague Convention signatory-country, the parents will should acquire a domestic study and work with an adoption company who is licensed in their country. And, of path, the kid will should be issued a visa by the State Department earlier than being allowed to go into the usa.

The Home Study

The organization or adoption company will provide you with the information of the home study. There is not any universally widespread layout for the house study so each

118

organization makes use of its personal. You can request an orientation on the method out of your agency, which is normally free and calls for no obligation for your part, so you can apprehend the things which might be required from the procedure as well as what kids are to be had from the enterprise and the way they work. In addition, many companies may additionally require the parents to go through education a good way to help them decide the sort of infant to adopt based on their parenting style and own family situations, as well as the child's wishes. In addition, they'll be familiarized with the requirements the employer imposes.

As potential parents, a social worker could be assigned in your case who will interview you numerous instances over the route of the adoption process with a view to better apprehend your unique family state of affairs. In addition to discussing the subjects in order to be included within the home observe, the social employee will also communicate to you about the kind of child that quality suits your family, which includes what traits you will be willing to just accept and if more than one placements (i.E. A sibling group) would be suitable. Among the topics with a purpose to probable be covered inside the interviews are: parenting style and your reviews with children, how you address pressure, how you're dealing with infertility in addition to other times of loss or crisis in your lifestyles. For couples, the interviews can be conducted mutually or on an individual basis, or each relying on what's deemed suitable through the social worker. The social worker might also interview grownup youngsters who are living out of doors of the family domestic.

If you already have kids, the social employee may also behavior interviews with them and can ask them to write a announcement approximately their own family life. As a part of the assessment, the social worker may even examine how they're doing in school and what their lifestyles is like at home. In addition, the social worker will also look at how they will deal with a new arrival within the own family, which includes having to share their dad and mom' time and attention.

As a part of the home have a look at, visits to your property could be performed. These visits are intended to assess your private home environment to make certain it's far a safe one for a kid and that it adheres to nation requirements (including providing ok living area for every toddler and having protection devices which includes smoke detectors mounted). In addition, your property need to be unfastened from potential risks (i.E. Toxic household chemicals ought to be saved accurately saved away in which the kid cannot attain them and firearms are kept in locked garage). To make certain that potential adoptive dad and mom have a look at those requirements, some states can also require that fire and fitness inspectors go to the home, further to the social worker's visits.

The social worker is needed to go through the entire residence with a view to see how you'll accommodate the brand new family member, looking at kids's bedrooms and regions that they frequent such as the outside and the basement. However, your house is not predicted to be impeccably orderly to skip those examinations, since the social employee is aware that a certain quantity of clutter accumulates around the residence throughout the method of daily living.

For global adoptions from Hague Convention international locations, the home take a look at has to fulfill certain requirements. These include the look at being performed by means of a identified service provider, what statements in your parenting eligibility are required to be protected in the take a look at and how they will be submitted to the relevant Central Authority for adoption in the country from which the child will come.

The simple information this is usually covered inside the home observe includes:

1.   Family history of the adoptive mother and father. What have been their childhoods like and how they have been parented? What is the repute in their beyond and present relationships with their dad and mom and siblings?

2.   Educational history. What instructional degree did they entire and what do they sense about their schooling? Do they plan to pursue better education inside the destiny?

three.   Employment. Where are the mother and father presently running? What is their status in their places of work? What is their beyond employment records?

4.   Relationship. If the adopting dad and mom are a couple, what's the fame of their relationship and their beyond history? If a unmarried individual is adopting, who're the

community of pals and own family who ought to assist them with a baby?

five.   Daily lifestyles. What is the day by day existence of the couple like? For a unmarried candidate, what is their social existence like and the way do they intend to modify their way of life to accommodate the adoptee?

6.   Neighborhood. Is the region wherein the potential dad and mom are living safe for youngsters? Is it near faculties and other community resources?

7.   Religious beliefs. Are the parents religious and what are their practices? What type of spiritual upbringing, if any, do they intend to provide the child?

eight.   Specific adoption troubles. Why do the candidates need to undertake? What type of baby do they agree with they might pleasant figure? If they already have youngsters, how do they intend to talk to them about the new family member and adoption in widespread? What degree of openness with the beginning parents might they experience cushty with?

nine.   The social employee's advice. This includes their assessment of your health to be adoptive parents as well as the encouraged kind and variety of kids for the family.

Other requirements consist of:

1. Health checks. Generally, potential mother and father are required to go through a bodily exam in addition to imparting a declaration from their health practitioner attesting to their good fitness and physical and mental fitness to determine a child. However, candidates with persistent health conditions along with hypertension and diabetes may additionally nevertheless be accredited for adoption as long as they are below control; people with more serious fitness problems, but, won't be authorised.

2. Income statements. Even if there's no minimal earnings requirement for adopting a toddler, potential dad and mom will still have to exhibit that they have the financial capability to attend to a infant. Generally, they will have to expose evidence of profits by using providing files together with numerous months' worth of pay slips, income tax returns for the past few years and W-four bureaucracy. In addition, precise organizations may additionally ask if the applicants have savings, insurance policies as well as how a good deal debt they're presently sporting.

3. Background assessments. All states require applicants to go through background

tests to see in the event that they have a record of baby abuse or a crook history, and relying on the legal guidelines of the nation, may be required to give Federal and State clearances as properly. Agencies are required to comply with kingdom and federal requirements regarding heritage checks and how the consequences of these can affect your eligibility to undertake. If there are particular incidents on your past that you agree with would possibly disqualify you from adopting, communicate together with your social worker approximately it since you could nevertheless be approved by way of the business enterprise relying on the nature of the incident and the way it become resolved.

4. Autobiographical statements. Many businesses might also require you to write down down an autobiography in order to permit your social worker to advantage a deeper information of you and your own family. Some groups may even ask you to create a scrapbook or album approximately your own family so that it will be provided to beginning parents to help them in considering if they'll area their baby with you. If you're interested in adopting older children, you may also be asked to prepare an album for them. If

you are having trouble writing approximately your self and your own family, your social worker might be capable of offer you with guide questions that will help you.

five.　　　References. You will usually be required to provide the names and contact information of at the least two or 3 humans now not related to you but who will act as your references. These people need to be individuals who are close to you and your own family, who have recognized you for some of years and feature visited your home and spent time with you and your own family. Suggested references may be your priest or rabbi, a beyond or cutting-edge employer, a colleague or a neighbor.

The procedure of finishing the house file will normally take around three to 6 months, relying on elements which include the variety of social employees assigned to you and how many different instances they'll be handling. To facilitate the technique, ensure that you complete all of the required office work to keep away from delays and assembly all of the requirements in a timely manner. Finally, hold in thoughts that you ought to usually be absolutely honest with your social worker. Never mislead them. If you have any concerns

126

that you believe may disqualify you, talk frankly to them approximately it. They is probably capable of discover a solution in order to let you remain qualified for adoption.

Helping Your New Child Adjust

Once you've got finished the adoption method, it's time to assist your new child or kids adapt to turning into part of your family. Of direction, this can not be a attention if you are adopting a new child, but in case you are taking in older children, the method of adjustment may be tough as they understandably experience tense approximately their new life occasions and how they can suit in. Keep in mind that those youngsters may have come from stricken backgrounds with a purpose to gift you with a completely unique set of demanding situations.

The Process of Adjustment

For instance, adoptive children can be afraid to turn out to be attached to their new circle of relatives out of fear that they could eventually be sent lower back to the orphanage or institution. The adoptive own family will must ensure that they sense welcomed and understand that they belong. They can also be feeling grief over being taken faraway from acquainted surroundings and those they'll have developed an attachment to, consisting of their caregivers.

In order to facilitate the procedure of adjustment, you'll must develop listening and conversation skills. When the kid talks, be an active listener, acknowledging what they're announcing by sending signals inclusive of nodding your head or saying k. This will help the adopted infant build shallowness by means of showing them that their emotions and evaluations are important and need to be heard. And when you have to talk with the child, you will have to learn how to send your message surely and with out ambiguity.

In addition, in case you are adopting a infant from overseas, you can help them alter by way of acknowledging their way of life and language instead of cutting them off from it in a mistaken notion that by way of doing so, it makes it simpler for them to acclimate to American subculture. You have to research the language of the child so that you can talk with them on account that they probably will now not realize how to speak English. You may additionally want to encompass a few factors in their culture of their room to lead them to experience more comfortable.

Another way you can help the child adjust is to undertake their preceding habitual as a part of your personal. For example, if the child ate lunch or dinner at a certain time at the same time as on the institution, you might consume your food on the identical time. You also can make the transition easier by cooking the kid's favourite food or serving his country's local delicacies.

It is likewise very vital that if you have kids, you furthermore may contain them in the method of adjustment. Hopefully, while the adopted baby comes domestic, you'll have already got had the difficult discussions with them about adoption. Even so, however, it is understandable if they're hesitant in together with the brand new toddler as a part of their lives. Don't force them to achieve this however as an alternative, let the bond between the kids expand evidently with the aid of encouraging them to spend time collectively. One manner you may do this is by way of establishing a circle of relatives culture which includes recreation night or movie night, or even some thing as simple as bedtime reading. These workouts can help the new infant greater without problems alter to the rhythms of his new family's life. Another way of fostering a sense of belonging in the new child is to create a family storybook which includes photographs and testimonies from the circle of relatives's beyond, and in order to sooner or later encompass the brand new toddler as a part of the own family history.

Another consideration is disciplining the adoptive child. Since they'll have come from an abusive background, you ought to area with care to illustrate which you aren't rejecting them. Some adoptive kids may carry out disruptive behaviors which include hoarding, lying, stealing and going into rages. One technique of disciplining an adoptive child showing disruptive conduct without reinforcing their feelings of rejection are 'sit down-ins' - you sit down down with the child and comfort them while they're raging.

Something to keep in mind isn't always to be too worried with small matters which include the manner they get dressed all through this period of adjustment. This can wait until later when the kid has come to be absolutely acclimated in your family.

Bonding Issues

130

When the kid first comes domestic, don't anticipate them to at once shape a bond together with your family. In reality, it is probably best if you don't weigh down them with interest once they first come home. If you are planning to keep a party for them, it's miles fine to wait till they have got adjusted before you achieve this.

You must additionally count on a piece of awkwardness as the kid is coming into a brand new international that is definitely unexpected to them and so they'll be withdrawn or even start crying. One manner you can help them alter is through displaying them physical affection through hugging them. At the begin, particularly if they are not used to it, the child may also stiffen or shrink back; but eventually, they will begin to reply.

Flexibility is likewise important since you should now not impose your expectancies on the kid at once. One of the worst things you may do is to force a parenting fashion on the child earlier than they display you who they're. For example, at the same time as American youngsters need their own space, a infant who comes from an organization wherein space turned into at a top rate might also in no way had been on their personal and be uncomfortable staying alone in their very own room. Thus, you have to adjust your parenting style based totally on the desires of the kid, in place of forcing the child to satisfy your style.

Another component to comprehend is that you can now not bond with the child at once. Often, when dad and mom are confronted with the reality of the kid being certainly found in the front of them, instead of seeing them in pics, they're surprised that there is no second of, "I fell in love with them without delay." That level of affection might also take time to broaden, but if you retain operating on it, that bond will ultimately expand. Many parents really file that they acted like they loved their new toddler for a long term before they absolutely commenced feeling that affection. This is something that adoptive mother and father are understandably hesitant to admit however which they need to well known that will address it.

Finally, don't hesitate to are seeking professional assist in case you want it. An skilled therapist who has familiarity with adoption issues can substantially help assist within the transition as well as helping the circle of relatives deal with different publish-

adoption problems. Many dad and mom have expressed regret that they did no longer are seeking counseling when they wished it, when you consider that it would have stored them a variety of grief that they might have avoided.

Chapter 8: Adoption Requirements

Who can Adopt?

Typically, any husband and spouse can mutually be eligible to adopt or a unmarried grownup can be eligible to undertake. A stepparent can undertake the delivery baby of his or her spouse. There are not any in addition conditions laid out in about 17 states and the District of Columbia. Some states do permit married people to adopt as a unmarried man or woman if they're legally separated from their spouse of if their spouse is not legally able.

In six states the age of adulthood for the purposes of adoption is 18. These states encompass:

• Kentucky
• Louisiana
• Montana
• New Jersey
• Tennessee
• Washington

In three states and American Samoa, the age of adulthood for the purpose of adoption is 21:

• Delaware
• Oklahoma
• Colorado

Georgia and Idaho specify the age of maturity for adoption as 25. There are a few states that do permit minors to adopt beneath precise situations, such as when the minor is the partner of the adult adoptive parent.

In 6 states and the Northern Mariana Island, the adopting mother and father have to be at the least 10 years older than the character to be followed:

• California
• Georgia
• Nevada
• New Jersey
• Utah
• South Dakota

In Puerto Rico, the adoptive parent must be at least 14 years older whilst in Idaho the adoptive discern need to be as a minimum 15 years older.

In approximately 17 states in addition to Guam, the Northern Mariana Islands, Puerto Rico and the Virgin Islands, petitioners for adoption are required to be state citizens. The required proof of residency levels from 60 days to one year. Some states do allow exceptions to the residency requirement under positive occasions, inclusive of with the adoption of a unique wishes baby.

Who can Adopt?

Generally, any grownup who could be considered a "healthy discern" is authorized to adopt a infant; however, in a few states there are special necessities for adoptive parents. For instance, a few states require adoptive parents to be a certain variety of years older than the adoptive child. Other states require adoptive dad and mom to be residents of that country for a specified quantity of time earlier than they will be allowed to undertake. If you intend to

136

undertake via an employer, you could additionally be required to satisfy in addition organization requirements, which can be typically stricter than kingdom legal guidelines.

It is not necessary in maximum times to be of the identical race as the kid you want to adopt, however in a few states choice is given to potential adoptive parents of the identical ethnic or racial background as the child. Adoptions of Native American youngsters are governed by means of federal regulation beneath the Indian Child Welfare Act. This act outlines particular methods and regulations that have to be accompanied while adopting a Native American infant.

Single Individuals

Single individuals may need to attend longer for an adoptive placement or be flexible regarding the child they adopt. Agencies regularly 'reserve' healthful toddlers in addition to younger children for 2-parent families, which can place unmarried individuals at the bottom of the waiting listing. In addition, birth mother and father

137

frequently desire for their youngsters to be placed in a -figure home.

If you're unmarried and desire to undertake, it's miles important to be organized to make an excellent case regarding your fitness as a parent. You must count on case people to question why you are not married, how you propose to guide and take care of the child, what's going to occur if you do marry in addition to different questions that could place you inside the position of defending your repute as a unmarried person. While this kind of screening may not seen fair, it could be fairly not unusual.

Agencies that serve children with special needs could be a great desire for unmarried people as they're frequently able to be extra bendy while considering adoptive parents. If you're bendy regarding your choices, it may make it less difficult to overcome any resistance you would possibly come upon regarding unmarried-determine adoptions.

Domestic Partners

There is not any specific prohibition in opposition to unmarried couples adopting

138

children. As is the case with single individuals, you would possibly discover that some agencies are biased in the direction of couples. You can also need to wait longer for a child or you can need to be greater flexible concerning the kid you are inclined to adopt.

Who may be Adopted?

All states as well as the District of Columbia and the U.S. Territories allow the adoption of a toddler; but, there are a few unique requirements that can follow in positive areas.

In 3 states in addition to the Northern Mariana Islands and American Samoa, the kid to be followed need to be below the age of 18. These states consist of Indiana, Colorado and Rhode Island.

In four states as well as Guam and American Samoa, the child have to be legally unfastened for adoption:

• Connecticut
• Delaware

- Montana
- Wisconsin

In six states, the Virgin Islands and American Samoa, it is required that the child to be followed need to be gift within the kingdom or territory at time the petition is filed:

- Arizona
- Colorado
- South Carolina
- Texas
- Wisconsin
- Wyoming

In Iowa it's far required that the kid have resided for not less than a hundred and eighty days in the domestic of the potential adoptive dad and mom.

There are also age requirements in a few states. In about 26 states and the District of Columbia, any character regardless of age is authorized to be adopted. Rhode Island, the Northern Mariana Islands and American Samoa permit individuals to petition the court docket for the adoption of people who're over the age of 18 however underneath age 21.

Nevada specifies that an grownup may be adopted ought to be younger than the adoptive parent. West Virginia allows a resident of that country handiest to undertake an person. Alabama restricts the adoption of adults to folks who're mentally retarded or permanently and absolutely disabled.

The adoption of an person is permitted in Ohio simplest while that individual is mentally retarded, completely disabled or a stepchild or foster infant with whom the connection become mounted whilst the child became a minor.

In Illinois, South Dakota and Idaho it is required that that the adopting determine be in a sustained parental courting for a certain period of time, which could variety from six months two years in order for an adult to be adopted.

Virginia allows the adoption of a niece, nephew or person stepchild so long as the adopted person resided within the domestic for at the very least three months earlier than accomplishing adulthood and is at least 15 years more youthful than the adopting discern.

Agency Adoptions
It may be beneficial to have your adoption managed via an employer for quite a few motives. Agencies are generally skilled in locating youngsters as well as matching them with mother and father and pleasurable the numerous necessary prison requirements. Agencies can help adoptive dad and mom with obligations from locating a birth figure to finalizing the adoption papers. An company can also cope with many other factors which are a part of the adoption system which includes conducting the house study, acquiring essential has the same opinion and advising dad and mom regarding any specific kingdom requirements.

Private and Public Agencies

The most important benefit to the usage of a personal organisation adoption is the quantity of counseling that a personal organization can offer. In maximum instances, counseling is available for birth mother and father, adoptive mother and father and the kids to be adopted if they may be antique enough. Counseling can help all of us involved with the emotional, practical and legal complexities that can come up for the duration of the adoptive procedure.

It is in particular critical for protection to be furnished to adoptive parents. In addition, a beginning figure who gets suitable counseling early within the method is likewise less in all likelihood to change her mind whilst the time involves sign the consent paperwork following the start of the toddler.

The disadvantage of using a non-public company is that such businesses can be quite selective with regard to selecting adoptive parents. This is due to the fact they frequently have greater mother and father who wish to adopt than the number of to be had children. As a end result, companies have a tendency to filter out dad and mom based on marital reputation, age, profits, sexual orientation, religion, fitness, non-public history and own family size.

Public groups however may additionally have extra kids who're geared up to be followed; however these kids are regularly special-needs or older youngsters. If you need to adopt a new child or an toddler, you may now not acquire a good deal help from a public agency. Public businesses typically do now not provide many different services, which includes the counseling that is supplied by private companies.

The gain of the use of a public business enterprise is that it could value less because there are fewer services offered. In fact, it may value you almost not anything to adopt via a public corporation. Some public businesses will even offer a small stipend for the duration of the adoption manner. In comparison, a personal organization adoption can cost heaps of dollars.

Keep in mind that in case you do pick out to apply an enterprise, you will maximum likely need to rent an attorney to draft the adoption petition and to represent you at some point of the technique. There isn't always surely a prison requirement that an lawyer be involved in the adoption; but, the procedure may be extremely complicated and ought to be handled with a person who has understanding and revel in in coping with adoptions. When hiring a lawyer, make certain you find out how many adoptions she or he has dealt with.

Agency Adoption Costs

Private agencies typically fee costs with a view to cowl the prices of the start mother which are allowed with the aid of nation. These prices can include scientific charges and dwelling prices at some stage in the being pregnant as well as counseling. When the body of workers salaries and overhead of the corporation are blanketed, prices can quickly upload up.

Many public agencies fee a flat charge for his or her adoptions, although some upload the beginning mother's expenses to the fixed charge this is charged for the corporation's services. Other agencies use a sliding scale that could vary according to the profits degree of the adoptive parents. You should count on to pay among $1,000 and $6,000 to adopt a young child and $10,000 or extra to adopt a new child thru a non-public enterprise. Some organizations will fee a lower fee for managing special wishes adoptions.

Public agencies normally do no longer fee fees for putting kids in adoptive homes.

Waiting Periods

Sometimes companies wait to area a child in an adoptive domestic until all of the vital is of the same opinion have been given in addition to finalized. Due to this, a child can be positioned in foster take care of a time frame, with the quantity of time relying upon the situation and the laws in that nation. Many adoptive parents are worried approximately the wait time after they wish for their toddler to have a steady and stable home as quick as feasible.

In some times, companies are able to get around this through setting babies right now in a form of adoption this is called a "legal danger placement". The chance comes from the truth that the birth mother may want to determine that she needs her child lower back before her felony rights were legally terminated. In that case, the adoptive parents will haven't any preference but to return the child.

Locating an Adoptive Agency

There are about 3,000 adoption corporations placed in the United States; public and personal. If you live in a kingdom consisting of New York or California you will have a long way extra alternatives than in case you stay in a kingdom this is less populated. Regardless of where you live, you may likely want to perform a little research as a way to locate an enterprise that meets your needs.

When thinking about an company, always make certain you check out the recognition of the company in addition to their accreditation. Begin with the licensing branch inside your country, which could inform you whether the organisation has been stated for any licensing violations and whether or not there were any lawsuits regarding that employer.

International Adoptions

An increasing number of American residents are actually looking to adopt youngsters. Due to the decreased range of youngsters that available for adoption within the United States, increasingly Americans are adopting youngsters from overseas international locations. This 12 months on my own, lots of youngsters will come to america; both followed whilst still abroad through U.S. Residents or as potential adoptees.

An international adoption is basically a non-public criminal count between a non-public person, or couple, who desires to adopt and a foreign court that operates below the laws and policies of that u . S .. U.S. Authorities are not able to interfere at the behalf of prospective mother and father in foreign courts in which the adoption occurs. The Department of State can offer facts regarding the adoption process in many nations in addition to the U.S. Felony necessities for bringing a infant that has been adopted abroad into america.

In order to finish an international adoption and produce a infant to america, prospective adoptive dad and mom must meet the requirements that are set up by means of the USA Bureau of Citizenship and Immigration Services in the Department of Homeland Security. Requirements of the foreign united states in which the kid resides, and once in a while requirements of the country of house of the adoptive mother and father, need to also be met. While techniques and documentary requirements can also seem repetitive, it's far vital to acquire numerous copies of every file in case they ought to be wished by means of BCIS, the overseas country or your house state.

The U.S. Immigration and Nationality Act (INA) is the U.S. Immigration law that deals with the issuance of visas to nationals of different nations, which incorporates youngsters which might be adopted abroad or come to the U.S. For adoption.

How the State Department can Help:

• Provide records about global adoption in international locations around the world
• Provide preferred facts about U.S. Visa necessities for worldwide adoption

• Make inquiries of the U.S. Consular phase overseas concerning the fame of a selected adoption case and clarify documentation or other necessities

• Ensure that U.S. Residents aren't discriminated in opposition to via overseas authorities or courts in accordance with neighborhood regulation on adoptions

What the State Department is Not Able to Do:

• Become at once concerned within the adoption manner in another country

• Act as an attorney or constitute adoptive parents in court

• Order that an adoption take region or that a visa be issued

While it is possible to undertake directly with an international adoption, most humans choose to apply an American employer that focuses on international adoptions due to the fact direct adoption from an global u . S . A . May be hard. The chance of problems with such direct adoptions may be in particular excessive. An company will apprehend the U.S. Immigration laws as well as the legal guidelines of the us of a in which the child is a resident along with the adoption legal guidelines of your nation.

Under U.S. Immigration legal guidelines, prospective adoptive dad and mom are required to be married or if they may be single they must be as a minimum 25 years vintage. Adoptive parents are required to document an Orphan Petition (Form I-six hundred) with the U.S. Citizenship and Immigration Services (USCIS, which become formerly referred to as INS). This is to demonstrate that the child's mother and father have died, disappeared or abandoned the kid and that any final figure isn't always capable of take care of the child as well as has the same opinion to the adoption and immigration of the child within the U.S. If there are known mother and father, the child will now not be eligible as an orphan, regardless of the occasions.

In addition to the Orphan Petition, adoptive mother and father will be required to put up several other documents, including a home observe record from the adoptive organization. If the petition is accredited via USCIS and there are not any disqualifying

151

factors inclusive of a communicable ailment, the child can be issued an immigrant visa.

Most of the office work for an global adoption can be finished earlier than the adoptive toddler has even been diagnosed. Advance education may be treasured because processing the office work can often be time ingesting and could genuinely postpone a toddler's arrival within the United States even after all the overseas requirements had been met.

It is imperative to make certain you check together with your country regarding any pre-adoption necessities. In a few states adoptive parents are required to submit written consent of the birth mother earlier than the entry of the kid into that country can be approved. In some times it's far vital to re-undertake a child; which may be required by way of the kingdom in that you stay or by way of the united states in that you adopted.

For greater facts about adopting a infant from a overseas us of a, contact:

International Concerns for Children

911 Cypress Drive
Boulder, CO 80303-2821
www.Iccadopt.Org

Independent Adoptions
There may be advantages and downsides to skipping the use of an organisation whilst adopting a baby.

An unbiased adoption may be appealing to both the beginning parents in addition to prospective adoptive parents because this kind of adoptive permits absolutely everyone concerned to maintain extra manipulate over the adoption manner. There are costs and risks worried with an unbiased adoption; but. In addition, adoptive parents must expect greater paintings in an adoption that does not contain an enterprise.

Advantages of Independent Adoptions

Some adoptive mother and father are reassured by means of in my opinion knowing the birth parents and being capable of address them immediately in place of being involved that the adoption ought to crumble before it is even finalized. Instead of counting on an enterprise to behave as a pass-among, in an unbiased adoption the delivery discern(s) and adoptive parents are capable of meet, get to understand one another and then decide for themselves whether or not they wish to proceed with the adoption. One of the advantages of an unbiased adoption is that it may assist adoptive dad and mom to keep away from the lengthy waiting lists in addition to the restrictive qualifying standards that could frequently be part of the usually company adoption.

Also, an independent adoption can frequently take area should quicker than an business enterprise adoption. In many instances, an impartial adoption can manifest within a 12 months of beginning the search for a infant. In addition, impartial adoptions can often be much less pricey than going thru an organisation. It must be stored in thoughts that adoptive dad and mom will nevertheless have most of the equal prices, inclusive of paying the charges of the beginning mom.

Disadvantages of Independent Adoptions

In many states significant restrictions are placed on independent adoptions. For instance, some states may restrict adoptive parents from marketing for a birth mom or might also restriction the amount of money that adoptive mother and father are able to contribute to the prenatal care of the delivery mom or her scientific costs.

Another issue related to an independent adoption is that the start mother and father won't get hold of appropriate counseling throughout the adoption system. States can fluctuate notably regarding the amount of counseling that is required for start parents before they make the very last choice to give up their infant for adoption. If the beginning determine(s) do not receive sufficient counseling, this can make the adoption agreement vulnerable.

In some states the period throughout which the parents might also revoke their consent in an independent adoption is extended. This can make it longer than the consent duration for an company adoption and could pose extra threat for the adoption settlement. If the adoption agreement ought to crumble, potential adoptive mother and father are at risk for losing full-size quantities of money and time and could don't have any recourse to be had to them.

Even when an independent adoption is a hit they may be numerous work. In most cases it's miles vital to lease an lawyer and even then there may be a whole lot of paintings worried. Adoptive mother and father can frequently spend big quantities of money and time in finding a delivery mom, further to the efforts which can be required to comply with through and finalize the adoption.

In a few states, Minnesota, Massachusetts, Delaware and Connecticut, independent adoptions are not prison. In these states it's miles feasible to behavior an enterprise directed adoption once you have got recognized birth mother and father. Make positive you take a look at your country laws.

Independent Adoption Costs

Every situation is distinctive, which means that that the costs for an unbiased adoption can broadly range. Prospective adoptive parents will typically be answerable for overlaying the costs of finding a delivery mother as well as the prices associated with the being pregnant and delivery in addition to costs worried with the criminal manner. Expenses inclusive of sanatorium bills, journey prices, phone bills, home take a look at charges, lawyer fees and court docket costs can regularly exceed $10,000. In some states, the adoptive parents are allowed to pay for the dwelling costs of the start mom as well.

All states permit adoptive dad and mom to pay reasonable costs are specifically adoption associated. It is illegal to buy or sell a infant in any nation; which means that each country has its personal laws that outline the prices that can be paid by means of adoptive parents in an adoption intending; whether it's far unbiased or organization. In an unbiased adoption, you're need to comply with these legal guidelines when providing any budget to the start mom. Most states do permit the adoptive parents to pay for the counseling clinical and attorney prices of the birth mom.

Most states require that any and all bills be itemized and accredited with the aid of the courtroom before the adoption can be finalized. Make certain you apprehend the laws of your country due to the fact both accepting or providing economic help this is prohibited can put you at hazard for crook fees. The adoption may also be at jeopardy if fallacious bills are made.

Open Adoptions

An open adoption is one wherein the adoptive parents and the delivery mother and father meet and then get to recognise each other prior to the adoption. Typically, all parties will attain an settlement with the beginning dad and mom keeping some level of contact with the child following the finalization of the adoption.

There is not any unmarried standard for open adoptions. Each circle of relatives normally works out an settlement with the intention to paintings for them. In some times, adoptive dad and mom will desire to satisfy the birth parents just once previous to the birth of the child. In other cases there is an ongoing relationship. In some instances, the contact is limited to the adoptive mother and father sending photos of the child regularly. In some instances, all events comply with normal visits among the kid and the start mother and father. While such visitation agreements are commonly a part of the prison proceedings for the adoption, they're not honestly enforceable by a courtroom. If the adoptive dad and mom do no longer stick to the agreement, there's generally now not a great deal the birth dad and mom can do.

The benefit to an open adoption is that it is able to help to limit the stress and worry. Adoptive parents can be reassured via for my part understanding the beginning mother and father as opposed to being afraid that a stranger will show up one day to satisfy their baby. This level of openness also can be beneficial to the kid as they may have fewer questions at the same time as growing up.

Just some many years ago, almost all adoptions had been closed. In a closed adoption there may be clearly no touch among the beginning parents and the adoptive parents once the adoption takes region. Today, there is an growing trend inside the U.S. Toward open adoptions.

159

Closed Adoptions

Today closed adoptions are uncommon. In a closed adoption, the adoptive parents typically area their name on a listing and await a fit to be made. The adoptive dad and mom will now not realize in which the child got here from or who the birth dad and mom are. The infant may also or may not even know that they were followed. In a closed adoption, the document is generally closed. Even if the adoptive mother and father and start dad and mom do recognise one another at the time of the adoption, they do now not live in contact once the adoption has been finalized.

The Home Study Process
In each nation in addition to the District of Columbia, prospective adoptive parents are required to take part in a domestic examine, irrespective of how they intend to adopt. There are 3 purposes to this process; to educate and put together the adoptive family for adoption, to gather facts approximately the own family to help a social employee in matching the circle of relatives with a baby

and to assess the adoptive circle of relatives for his or her fitness as adoptive mother and father.

For some adoptive dad and mom, the home take a look at can be a source of hysteria as they'll be involved they may no longer be accepted. It may be beneficial to preserve in thoughts that organizations are not looking for perfect mother and father. Instead, they're looking for dad and mom who can meet the needs of the kid they're matched with.

The precise requirements for the home examine process can vary extensively from enterprise to company in addition to from nation to country.
There isn't always a hard and fast layout that agencies use for accomplishing home research. In many organizations the subsequent steps are used for their home examine procedure; despite the fact that the details can vary.

Training

Many businesses require potential parents to wait schooling either prior to or for the duration of the house have a look at method. Such training facilitates potential dad and mom to better apprehend the needs of the kids which are waiting to be adopted whilst additionally helping households to determine which kind of infant they may be capable of maximum efficiently discern.

Interviews

It isn't unusual for potential parents to be interviewed several instances with the aid of a social employee for the duration of the house examine procedure. These interviews will assist parents to develop a courting with the social worker with a purpose to handle the adoption manner and enable him or her to better recognize the circle of relatives and assist to make the maximum suitable placement.

Home Visit

A home go to serves the primary reason of ensuring the house of the adoptive mother and father meets state licensing requirements, together with working smoke alarms, secure storage of firearms, secure water and good enough area for the child.

In addition, most corporations do require prospective adoptive mother and father to have a few type of bodily examination. This is critical as a critical fitness trouble ought to have an effect on the life expectancy of the parents and will prevent approval.

While you do not ought to be wealthy so that you can adopt, you do need with a view to reveal which you are able to manipulate your finance responsibly and accurately. Typically, prospective dad and mom are required to verify their earnings via providing copies of pay stubs, earnings tax bureaucracy, and so forth.

Most states additionally require crook history tests for all adoptive and foster parent applicants. This can also encompass a fingerprint historical past test.

An autobiographical declaration is likewise required through many adoption businesses. The is largely a life story that will help the social worker to higher understand the circle

163

of relatives and help them in writing the home look at report.

The organisation may ask for the names and phone records of several people who can serve as references for the adoptive dad and mom. References assist the social employee to set up a more entire picture of the own family and their help network.

All of these steps commonly culminate in writing the home take a look at document on the way to reflect the finding of the social paintings. The home have a look at report may be used to introduce the adoptive own family to other businesses or adoption exchanges to assist in matching the circle of relatives with a child expecting adoption.

Generally, domestic study reviews include the above mentioned statements, heritage checks and reference further to the subsequent:

- Family historical past
- Education/employment
- Relationships
- Daily lifestyles
- Parenting

- Neighborhood
- Religion
- Feelings approximately/readiness for adoption

Top Ways for Locating a Child Available for Adoption

There are many exclusive ways you could discover a infant who's available for adoption. Below are some of the maximum common methods.

Friends, Relatives and Co-people

When you are prepared to undertake, make sure you get the word out and permit others recognise you are making plans to undertake a baby. Many connections have been made clearly via word of mouth.

Churches and Other Places of Worship

Religious companies regularly have connections to other agencies; both international and home and may be able to find out about youngsters who are in want of an adoptive circle of relatives.

Advertise

As a end result of the shortage of infants who are available for adoption within the United States, some individuals and couples have chosen to take a more particular method to finding a infant; which could consist of advertising in the newspaper, in magazines and even on billboards.

Internet

The Internet has opened a very new network for acquiring information about adoption. It can be a fantastic start line for gaining knowledge of about adoption sources and connecting with birth parents.

Attorneys

Lawyers who specialize in adoption and own family law can often be a excellent supply of leads as well. Such legal professionals have established a ways attaining connections that can help in figuring out a toddler who's to be had for adoption or for connecting prospective adoptive mother and father with start dad and mom, often even earlier than

166

the child is born. Once a beginning mother or baby has been located, the legal professional can lead you through the paperwork, file the desired courtroom files, represent you in court and make certain that the entirety is successful.

Surrogacy

Another option that some dad and mom keep in mind is surrogacy. This association involves creating a settlement with every other girl to hold a child to term. The woman will then relinquish custody of the kid at once after delivery. In some instances the surrogate will bring a infant that changed into conceived via the usage of sperm from the prospective father. In that case, he is the legal father and most effective the possible mother will want to undertake the kid after beginning. In different cases, the child is not biologically related to both of the mother and father and both will want to adopt the child after beginning.

Foster Parenting

Serving as a foster discern also can cause a a hit adoption. Unfortunately, many foster mother and father will set up deep bonds with the kids they foster and can attempt to undertake them; simplest for the children to be returned to their delivery households or later adopted by means of a person else. In many cases; however, foster parenting can cause the a hit adoption of a foster toddler. At the least, serving as a foster figure will assist you to play an important function in a child's life and provide you with the opportunity to improve your parenting competencies even as preparing for adoption. Foster parenting can also help you to emerge as familiar with humans who may be capable that will help you in finding a baby to be had for adoption.

County and Government Organizations

There are a few neighborhood government gadgets which could help with adoptions as nicely. There are many kids within the foster care machine who are awaiting adoptive families and working with a neighborhood government unit may be capable that will help you emerge as matched with a toddler. Some foster care programs will host social

168

activities wherein potential adoptive parents and kids to be had for adoption can meet one another.

Doctors

Your medical doctor and different doctors also can serve as right sources for adoption referrals. Family practitioners and obstetricians regularly have touch with unmarried mother and can understand a beginning mom who has decided to area her child for adoption.

Adoption Agencies

Many prospective parents and delivery dad and mom paintings with certified adoption agencies. Such companies are occasionally able to in shape adoptive mother and father and birth mother and father. Prospective adoptive mother and father may also place their records in a ebook that can be reviewed by way of start parents who will then pick the family wherein they would really like their toddler to be placed.

Adoption Cost Facts

Often, potential adoptive parents may be involved regarding the financial expenses related to adopting a infant and their capability to fulfill those fees. Although giving birth to a infant can be rather inexpensive when you have adequate insurance coverage, adopting a child can gift preliminary prices that may be challenging. Advance planning and expertise concerning the one of a kind types of adoptions and the resources which might be available can assist prospective adoptive parents to increase a finances on the way to encompass most of the foreseeable charges.

The overall cost of adoption can vary from nothing to extra than $40,000, depending on a range of of factors. Below is a chart that outlines a number of the more trendy adoption prices. The extensive variety in charges reflects the range of factors that could affect adoption charges which include the form of agency placement, the type of adoption the kid's age and different occasions.

Adoption Costs

Foster Care Adoptions $0 to $2,500

Licensed Private Agency Adoption $5,000 to $40,000+
Independent Adoptions $8,000 to $forty,000+
Facilitated/Unlicensed Adoptions $5,000 to $40,000+
Intercountry Adoptions $7,000 to $30,000

Universal Costs

Universal prices are the ones prices which might be incurred by every body who adopts a toddler. These fees consist of domestic study costs and courtroom expenses.

Home Study Expenses

A home examine ought to be finished for all prospective mother and father no matter the sort of adoption they intend to complete. The cause of the house observe is to prepare the possible dad and mom for adoption as well as gather facts about the circle of relatives so the best suit can be made. The price for the home examine is usually paid through the possible adoptive parents. In the case of a foster care adoption, there can be no charge

171

for engaging in the home have a look at. Parents might also incur costs for mental or scientific opinions that may be required as part of the technique; however.

In different forms of adoption, the non-public organization or a licensed or licensed social employee may also price as much as $three,000 for the house observe. A price for the house take a look at may be covered inside the average business enterprise rate in a few cases.

Legal Fees

All domestic adoptions and some global adoptions must be finalized in a court docket within the United States. Some international adoptions can be finalized within the infant's country of starting place. Although it is not required in all conditions, adoptive parents may also select to finalize the location in a U.S. Court to reap extra protection in their infant's felony popularity. Such procedures do incur a value. The price for court document practise can range as much as $2,000. The fee for prison representation can range from $1,000 or greater. In the case of a foster care adoption, a few states provide repayment for legal prices to the adoptive mother and father.

Adoption Specific Expenses

Along with the costs which can be widely wide-spread to each adoption, adoptive parents may incur prices which can be unique to their form of adoption. There are 3 simple sorts of adoption; foster care, home toddler and global.

Domestic Infant Adoption Costs
This sort of adoption can value from about $five,000 to $40,000 or greater. The charges can range extensively based at the type of organisation used and in some instances the person adoption instances. It is vital for prospective adoptive dad and mom to make sure they absolutely understand what is covered in each the enterprise and legal professional costs. The home study can be included in the price in a few cases.

There are three popular categories for domestic infant adoptions. They are:

• Licensed Private Agency Adoptions

o This form of domestic infant adoption can value $five,000 to $forty,000 or greater. The fees for this form of adoption consist of a rate that is charged with the aid of the company in conjunction with the value of the home study, adoptive determine coaching and education, beginning discern counseling and social paintings services.

• Independent Adoptions

o This kind of home little one adoption can value from around $8,000 to $40,000, with an average of round $12,000. An impartial adoption is normally treated by an legal professional and may consist of such fees as medical charges as allowed by using regulation for the delivery mom, prison fees for representation of the birth mother and the adoptive mother and father and some other allowable costs, including advertising.

• Facilitated/Unlicensed Agency Adoptions

o The value for this sort of adoption can variety among $five,000 to $40,000 and will commonly encompass the identical prices as that of a certified enterprise adoption.

International Adoptions

The charges for this form of adoption can range between $7,000 and $30,000. Agencies that provide global adoption services can fee costs for offerings such as file and immigration processing and courtroom charges. It might also include a required donation to the foreign business enterprise or orphanage. The universal costs for this kind of adoption can be affected based on the sort of entity in the foreign united states of america that is responsible for placement of the kid; along with whether or not it's far a central authority orphanage, authorities corporation, charitable basis, and so forth.

Agencies that offer intercountry adoption services rate expenses that range from $7,000 to $30,000. These costs typically include dossier and immigration processing and court costs. In a few instances, they may include a required donation to the foreign orphanage or business enterprise. Overall charges may be tormented by the kind of entity within the overseas u . S . A . This is accountable for putting the child (e.G., authorities organisation, government orphanage, charitable basis, attorney, facilitator, or a few combination thereof). Many intercountry adoption companies provide a sliding fee scale.

Depending on the united states of america, there could be additional costs, including:

• Child foster care (common in South and Central American adoptions)
• Parents' tour and in-usa live(s) to manner the adoption overseas
• Escorting fees, charged whilst dad and mom do no longer journey but as an alternative hire escorts to accompany the child at the flight
• Child's medical care and remedy (now and again in South and Central America)
• Translation costs
• Foreign lawyer costs
• Foreign enterprise costs
• Passport fees
• Visa processing prices
• Costs for visa scientific exam

Questions To Ask Your Child's Caseworker
After your private home observe has been completed and you have expressed interest in a specific baby, you may usually have the risk

to speak to the child's caseworker at the side of in all likelihood other human beings worried within the baby's life. Asking questions will give you an opportunity to better apprehend what it will be want to parent that baby.

In any sort of adoption, whether it's miles an business enterprise adoption, impartial, home or overseas adoption, it is essential to achieve as a lot accurate genetic, medical and social history as possible approximately the possible child. There is a sure degree of chance concerned in adoption; however, history facts can be useful for the following reasons:

It makes it viable for the prospective dad and mom to make an informed decision concerning accepting a infant. When you have an accurate and complete know-how of a infant's needs earlier than placement, you'll be better capable of determine whether or not your family can be capable of take care of the child, consisting of whether or not you have the economic and emotional sources to satisfy the desires of that child.

It permits you to get right of entry to federal or nation adoption subsidies that can be available for kids with unique wishes. Adoption subsidies, also every now and then called adoption assistance, can be to be had for youngsters with special desires. Not all youngsters will first-class for such subsidies. Special wishes can also consist of children with medical desires and children who could be greater hard to region in an adoptive own family because of their age, because they're part of a sibling organization and/or due to their race or ethnicity.

Background records additionally offers an opportunity for the kid to broaden an correct sense in their records. Without the presence of accurate records, adopted youngsters can expand fantasies approximately their records which are unrealistic. They may also sense disconnected from their beyond.

In addition it gives an opportunity for early diagnosis in addition to remedy and intervention for developmental troubles and conditions. Knowledge of clinical problems in a baby's birth circle of relatives can offer the capability to offer treatment greater quickly.

You can attain historical past facts by way of contacting neighborhood groups and asking about the kinds of children that employer commonly locations and the standard backgrounds of these youngsters. Remember that each infant is an person and has the potential to have their very own particular troubles. Agencies will commonly percentage extra precise facts about a infant as soon as the own family has completed a home take a look at and has expressed an hobby in adopting that unique toddler.

National online adoption groups as well as image listings can provide preferred descriptions in addition to photographs of youngsters who're waiting to be followed. The descriptions in picture listings tend to be quick so it's miles essential to recognize what can be meant with the aid of certain phrases. For example, a description like "very active, needs quite a few attention, impulsive" could mean the kid has been diagnosed with Attention Deficit Disorder. A baby that is defined as "developmentally delayed" might

also had been recognized with slight to mild intellectual retardation. It is essential to be alert to any terms that might indicate what it might be want to figure that toddler. After your private home examine has been finished, talking with the kid's caseworker along side former instructors and foster parents can come up with a clearer idea.

The questions you ask and the data you are capable of acquire will often be based totally on the kid's age, as a minimum to some degree. In the example of an little one the birth determine's health history, specially the prenatal care of the start mother might be in particular essential. In the case of an older baby you may want to reap extra comprehensive statistics inclusive of social, developmental, mental fitness and educational histories. In the event the kid has been in foster care, then certainly the questions you'll want to invite may be greater complex.

• What might a toddler with this records accept as true with about him/herself?

• What could a baby with this history trust about mother and father/caretakers/the sector?
• What kinds of behaviors must I anticipate from a child with this records?
• What unique competencies, talents, or assets is probably important to determine this specific toddler (e.G., medical understanding or abilities, handy housing, special cultural or parenting training)?

Questions Regarding your Child's Medical and Family History

• How complete is the social/clinical history at the beginning own family, together with extended circle of relatives? What is lacking? Is it viable to get more information?
• What is the birth own family's racial, ethnic, cultural, and spiritual heritage?
• What is the general physical description of the child's birth dad and mom, siblings, and different close spouse and children? Are there pictures? (Attempt to get snap shots of a toddler's birth parents and spouse and children on every occasion viable, due to the fact this could enable you to reply the questions often asked with the aid of adopted

181

youngsters: "What did my birth mother and father appear like?" or "Who do I appear like?")

• Is there a family history of drug or alcohol abuse?

• Is there a circle of relatives history of intellectual contamination or other genetic situations, or predispositions to sicknesses which include diabetes or heart disorder?

• What was the age and purpose of loss of life of close relatives within the beginning family?

• What is known approximately the beginning discern's developmental records-physically, emotionally, cognitively, consisting of language development?

• What is understood approximately the academic historical past of the beginning dad and mom and the kid's siblings?

• What are the special capabilities, skills, skills, or interests of delivery dad and mom and family participants?

• Are there letters, snap shots, videotapes, and presents from the start own family?

• What changed into the delivery mother's fitness like for the duration of pregnancy, and what changed into the health of each parent on the time of the kid's beginning?

• What prenatal care did the kid get hold of, and what was his or her situation at delivery?

• When did he or she reap developmental milestones, and feature there been any developmental exams reflecting deviation from traditional improvement?

• Are there prior clinical, dental, psychological, or psychiatric examinations and/or diagnoses for this baby?

• Are there facts of any immunizations and/or health care obtained at the same time as the kid become in out-of-domestic care?

• What is the kid's modern-day need for scientific, dental, developmental, psychological, or psychiatric care?

• What is the child's HIV popularity?

Questions Regarding your Child's Social and Placement History

• Why did the beginning dad and mom make an adoption plan for the child, or why was the kid removed from his or her beginning circle of relatives?

• Did the child go through any physical, sexual, or emotional abuse or overlook? At what point inside the toddler's existence did

183

she or he experience these traumas? How frequently? By whom?

• How many placements did the child have, and in which (e.G., relative placements, foster houses, orphanages, residential treatment facilities, hospitals)? What had been the motives for placements or re-placements? What does the kid bear in mind about his or her placements? What does the child accept as true with about why he or she became positioned or moved from one placement to every other? (The child's perception may also or might not be correct, but it is critical to apprehend a child's notion of his or her placement records.)

• Where is the child presently enrolled and what is his or her performance at school?

• What are the effects of any academic testing and are there any special instructional desires?

• Are there full-size occasions (early separations, multiple caretakers, abuse/forget) inside the baby's lifestyles that might affect his or her potential to relate to a brand new own family?